THE
ROBERT OLEN BUTLER
PRIZE STORIES
2004

THE
ROBERT OLEN BUTLER
PRIZE STORIES
2004

DEL SOL PRESS

The Robert Olen Butler Prize Stories 2004

Copyright © 2005 by Del Sol Press. All rights reserved.

DEL SOL PRESS, WASHINGTON, D.C.
Paper ISBN: 0-9748229-5-7

FIRST EDITION

COVER PHOTOGRAPH COURTESY OF MICHAEL NEFF

COVER & INTERIOR DESIGN BY ANDER MONSON.

Publication by Del Sol Press/Web del Sol Association, a not-for-profit corporation under section 501 (c) (3) of the United States Internal Revenue Code.

❧ Contents ☙

❧ *Acknowledgments* ❧

Thanks to the following magazines, in which the following stories originally appeared.

Thomas P. Balázs, "Omicron Ceti III," *Big City Lit*
Ariana-Sophia Kartsonis, "Sundress," *Glimmer Train*
Roy Kesey, "Invunche y Voladora," *Nimrod*
Dylan Landis, "Jazz," *Tin House*
Kelly Magee, "Not People, Not This," *Quarterly West*
Lynn Veach Sadler, "Miss Spam Maps of Vegas," *Mississippi Review Online*
Marianne Taylor, "Who Is the Hardware," *Dogwood Literary Journal*
Charles Yu, "My Last Days as Me," *Sou'wester*

❦ *The 2004 Prize Winner* ❧

❧ *News from My Father* ❧

E. R. CATALANO

On Saturday nights we said the rosary. My mother, my aunts, and me. I would kneel in front of a small table on which stood my father's picture, a Hollywood head shot surrounded by candles. Over the sound of our voices we could hear the traffic on the street; a truck on its way to the highway would lumber down our block rattling all the windows of our second-floor apartment, or the guy with the homemade motorcycle would tear past, setting the neighbor's dog to barking.

My mother stood behind me, her right hand on my shoulder, like Confirmation two years before. I could smell her perfume, Shalimar, thick as incense. On the couch behind us my aunts said the rosary with us, although once in a while I heard heavy breathing coming from Aunt Tess so I knew she'd fallen asleep. Except for the candles, the only other light came from a lamp in the corner, turned to its lowest setting. This was my mother's idea of a séance.

There are two stories in my family, often retold, concerning my great-grandmother's ability to see the dead. In the first she has just turned fifteen, a peasant girl living in turn-of-the-century

Naples; she is hanging up clothes to dry one afternoon when she sees a friend pass by in the street. The girl calls to her in greeting before continuing on her way, and then my great-grandmother finishes her chores. Later, she learns that the girl had drowned in the river the previous night.

When I was younger I enjoyed this story for the chill it would inspire. I imagined my great-grandmother to be Sophia Loren, a kerchief tied around her hair to keep back loose strands while she hangs sheets, her mind preoccupied with thoughts of a man, not the man she is to marry within the year. She is so deep in her fantasy that she barely notices when the village girl walks by. The part of the story where she finds out that the girl had already been dead for hours when she saw her is never dramatized. It would just hang there like a finger about to slide down your spine. So I added the scene:

That night, helping her mother set the table for dinner, she looks up as her father enters, bringing with him news of the girl's death. Then, my great-grandmother, her hair falling from her kerchief and her eyes wide with shock, bites her knuckle until she draws blood.

The second story takes place ten years after the first. In this one her unique gift saves her life and the lives of her family. My great-grandmother was married and had five children by the time she was twenty-five. One night as they sleep a fire starts in the house. It would've killed all of them if not for my great-grandmother's dream. In this dream a friend of the family, who had died just days before, tells her to wake up and get her family out of the house. The vision is so clear she jumps out of bed whereupon she smells the smoke and wakes her family, saving them in time. When I was younger I believed the second was the better of the two stories. I now prefer the first because I know it's just like life to have a psychic gift that tells you nothing.

We sat around the table, long after dinner, cracking nuts, and my mother and her two sisters told me my great-grandmother had this ability because words were left out of her baptism. Which words and why? My aunts and mother shushed me.

"Have some respect, Martina," they said.

But I muttered that the details were sketchy. And besides, I had a personal stake.

When I was born my mother had promised Father Sal to add her deep alto to the church choir for the rest of her life on this earth if he would leave words out of my baptism. Which words and why? Unimportant, she told him, just a few words, a sentence maybe. He agreed, but I had reached the age of fourteen without seeing even one ghost. No specters either. No strange noises. No pages of an open book turned by an unseen hand. Not even so much as a premonition. But my mom held out hope. What she hoped for was a word from Dad. Their life together had broken in a bad place and she needed closure.

Martin Coreo, my father, had been a salesman traveling up and down the East Coast selling ad space in a national trade magazine. One night, when my mother was a couple of months pregnant with me, he called her from a roadside rest stop in Georgia and they ended up having a fight because he was supposed to be on his way home, and Savannah was nowhere near Queens. He ran out of change and said he'd call her back, but he never did. Driving north through South Carolina, he fell asleep at the wheel, drove the car into a ditch, and broke his neck.

My Aunt Tess told me that my mother held his road map of Georgia clasped to her heart for the duration that I was tucked under it. Until I was five years old my mother used to press the map into my hands, hoping that he'd complete the journey begun on interstate highways and local roads to come back to her.

By the time I was fourteen I had become tired of seeing the

expectant look on my mother's face every time I sneezed or hiccuped. When it didn't happen as a child, my mother thought maybe it would happen when my periods started. After all, my great-grandmother was fifteen the first time she saw the dead.

She took to preparing me. She told me of the cramps and headaches she used to get, and how in her day they didn't have sanitary napkins, just special underwear they had to wash out every day. I didn't want to hear this. If I couldn't see *her* as Sophia Loren, I at least wanted to imagine myself that way.

My mother's looks were what people would call striking. Her long dark hair was shot through with gray and she did not color it. This made her appear dramatic, ageless. At the bank where she worked as a teller, and even at home, she kept her hair sharply pulled back from her face, emphasizing high cheekbones, which I did not inherit.

She was always cooking. Sauce simmered on the stove. Grain pie cooled in the refrigerator. Slices of eggplant dried between paper towels in long rows on the counter. Or she was reading. She'd sit in the kitchen alternately reading and watching the stove. She read biographies of dead historical figures. She didn't use bookmarks and she wouldn't dog-ear pages; she always knew where she'd left off. She wore black forever after my father died.

When my aunts visited they would look me over and comment on how I was getting breasts, a term which had embarrassed me ever since I was seven and a girl from down the block had pulled up the tank top of her Barbie doll, pointed and told me, "tits." When I repeated the word in front of my mother, she smacked me in the back of the head and told me never to use that word again. She said the right word was "breasts," but my impression was it would be best to avoid referring to them at all. I wasn't satisfied with either designation, just as I wasn't satisfied with my own breasts, which were barely there, and I was even less

happy with my aunts' remarks about my burgeoning development.

"They're small now, Marty, but wait till you have children. Then
they'll be bigger," Aunt Sylvia said.

My mother said, "Let her grow up first and get married."

Then my Aunt Tess leaned into me. "Don't worry. It's okay to
be small. Look at me."

Within everything lurks the potential to embarrass a fourteen-
year-old. I had braces. I had glasses. I had allergies. Every time I
blew my nose my mother would raise her eyes from hemming
one of my skirts for school and say, "The horn works, now try the
lights." Sophia Loren's mother would never have said that to her.
Some things said by family cut off all hope of your ever being
sexy or mysterious, would keep you from becoming a glamorous
woman with secrets and a lustrous mane of hair falling from beneath a kerchief. Instead I was stuck being a fourteen-year-old
girl struggling with allergies and small breasts in a room clut-
tered with packages of tissues while waiting for her period.

When it came I decided to tell my mother as nonchalantly as
possible. Actually, while she was on the phone with my Aunt
Sylvia. I could hear my aunt on the other end yelling, "Flora? Has
she got her period? What did Martin say?"

Every twenty-eight days I had cramps and headaches, as awful as my mother's used to be, and this was when she wanted me
to listen especially hard for my father's voice. Then her sisters
reminded her of how my great-grandmother used to wear her
nightgown backwards when she wanted to communicate with
the dead. The rationale, apparently, was that things got tired of
going forward all the time so you needed to show you were ready
to accept them the opposite way. I could try to just think of my
father, but a physical sign was recommended. To me it seemed
like people listening to records backwards to hear hidden mes-

sages from Satan. Also, I figured if dead people came knocking on my bedcovers it would most likely be to tell me that my pajamas were on the wrong way.

Once a month I took the day off from school and spent it doubled over in my bed. Although my mother commiserated with me, she refused to buy me painkillers, claiming that every psychic journey began with pain. Sometimes my friend Julie came over smuggling Midol in her purse and we'd discuss which boys we liked—Jimmy Dunlevy and Javier Sanchez—which girls we didn't—Tricia Keeling—and whether Ms. Walker, the gym teacher, was a lesbian.

I knew I was strange compared to the other girls at St. John's. I wasn't allowed to wear makeup. I went to church at least once a week and sometimes more. No Midol allowed. Preferred pads to tampons. Had latent ability to see the dead. Wore bells of leper.

Three of my cycles went by and there was still no sign I could commune with the dead. We sat at the table after dinner one Saturday night, my mother attempting to extract Brazilian nuts whole from their shells. She'd get one open, then it would break apart, so she'd discard it uneaten and start on another.

I had been meaning to ask her if I could go to the church dance at the end of the month and in the silences in between the nut-cracking it seemed as good a time as any, so I did, knowing what her answer would be, but that at least I could tell Julie I had asked.

"No, Martina," she said.

"Why not?"

She waved the nutcracker in an indeterminate circle. "You are too young yet." I sighed and she returned to her work, again breaking the nut before she could remove the shell.

My Aunt Tess said something like, just like *you*, they're hard nuts to crack, and Aunt Sylvia chuckled and my mother smiled and I, amazed by my mother's good humor at being teased or perhaps just relieved that my headaches and cramps were ended for another month, let my guard down and laughed with my mouth wide open and my head thrown back. My mother turned to me and said, "If you're not careful the devil's going to take advantage of the entrance you're offering and dive right in."

Soon after, the Saturday night rosary sessions began.

It can take a long time to say the rosary. Bead after bead itches through your fingers until you feel swallowed up in time. Saying the rosary is supposed to smooth the ripples, get you ready to accept. A spiritual and physical exercise, keeping your mind and hands busy so that the soul can come on through. As always, my mother stood behind me, her hand on my shoulder. Perhaps she wanted to be linked to me so that if Dad didn't recognize his daughter kneeling in his old living room, he might recognize his wife standing behind her.

The Hail Marys bled into each other. Each recitation sounded five words long yet the decades seemed to take decades until we capped them off with Our Fathers and their corresponding larger beads.

I contemplated lying to my mother about seeing my dad just so she would leave me alone, leave off these Saturday nights telling me to make my mind blank while I concentrated on a face I'd never seen in life. I planned to tell her that Dad had appeared to me to say he hated her and had been preparing to leave her. Furthermore, as he didn't know me, he preferred to talk to me instead of her anyway. Then she'd realize her selfishness, fall to her knees and beg for my forgiveness. She'd see it was one thing to ruin her own life waiting for a sign but another to ruin her daughter's.

The light from the candles made me drowsy. Perhaps it was supposed to hypnotize me, fill in the blanks I would be unable to fill in with my conscious mind. I'd see Dad, say hello, ask did he miss us? But my mind only wandered, occasionally hitting on random acts of violence. Knocking over the candles, holding one to my mother's throat, keeping the aunts at bay. I had to fight the urge to laugh. Then I wondered if my father would be mad, or if he would laugh too.

Afterwards, we would watch a rented movie that my aunts brought. And as I sat there on the floor in front of these women, my family, I wished myself to be any of the characters in the movie, comic or tragic, just to escape this religious hysteria.

On the night of the dance, I looked in the drawer by my mother's bedside where she kept his road maps. I took them to my room, placed a chair in front of the door, and spread the map of Georgia out on the bed. I examined it for pencil marks, trying to discern places he might've visited, might've liked, where maybe he'd sold some ad space and had a hamburger. I used to believe he had been having an affair and had faked his own death in order to be with this other woman and his other daughter because life with my mother had been unsatisfactory. Rosaries every Saturday night were not his idea of a good time. A man like my father needed more than spiritual fulfillment. And I was my father's daughter.

When my mother eventually called me to prayer, I folded the maps, slipped into her room, and returned them to the bottom of her drawer.

In the middle of that night's rosary, my mind wandered to Jimmy Dunlevy and how right at that moment Tricia Keeling might be slow dancing with him. And here I was, locked in this strange inanimate dance with my mother and aunts, all this dim lighting being wasted. My fifteenth birthday was approaching and I still hadn't kissed anyone.

My mother pressed my shoulder. I had stopped praying. I muttered an apology and continued on. Aunt Tess was in deep hibernation. Aunt Sylvia had probably replaced her rosary beads with the *TV Guide* and was whispering the movie-of-the-week instead of the Our Father. We were starting the third decade, more than the rest of my life yet to go.

Fixating on the candle in front of me I half closed my eyes and pictured Jimmy Dunlevy. Jean jacket always falling off one shoulder or the other, blond bangs coming to a jagged halt above his eyelashes, a cigarette balanced between his lips. The week before I made Julie go out into the blighted courtyard outside the cafeteria so we could pretend to be getting air, a dubious prospect among all the smokers. Julie said I should ask Jimmy for a cigarette. That would get his attention. Only I was against smoking. Open quote, it was a dirty and disgusting habit, close quote. But this wouldn't stop me from getting as close to him as I dared. Our approach and then last-minute avoidance of danger lets us know we're alive. I wasn't going to jump out of an airplane, I was just going to get close to a boy with an attitude and breathe in his secondhand smoke. In the end I stood a few feet away while Julie went up to his friend Dave and bummed a cigarette off him. Jimmy's eyes passed over me briefly.

Just then homemade motorcycle guy roared down the block. The windows rattled, which startled my Aunt Tess into waking. I imagined running to the window and saying, "That must be Dad now." My mother cleared her throat and continued praying. We were up to an Our Father, but I was still doing a Hail Mary. I looked down at my hand and sure enough between my thumb and forefinger was one of the larger beads. My hands were starting to feel sore and clammy. Holding the beads was too subtle a muscular process for the hands to be comfortable. And the carpet was too thin for my knees. Again this week I would have welts on them that would take hours to fade.

If only my father would appear to tell me I didn't have to do this anymore, or that there was some point to it all. Julie had asked me what I did on Saturday nights. Why didn't my mom let me go to dances or parties? Was I to tell her the truth? It was my father. He might want to talk. Wasn't he dead? Yes, why do you ask? Meanwhile my knees ached and the carpet itched my shins. C'mon, Dad, let's go, my legs hurt. If I could just take a break, I thought. Just five minutes. I contemplated the baptism of five minutes. Then I thought of water, of being immersed in water. Then I thought of Jimmy Dunlevy, because I would've liked to be immersed in water with him. Because that seemed like a good idea. Before I knew it I was in the cafeteria and Jimmy's smoke was fresh on my sweater and I kept bringing the collar up to my nose. (I'd folded the sweater I'd worn that day in the courtyard and put it in the bottom of my drawer as soon as I came home from school so I could trap his smell, so I could be reminded of him anytime.) Now, I breathed deeply, thinking of the dangers of adulthood, the dark burning future, the endless horizons, the possible emphysema.

At this moment I knew he was dancing with someone else. And it was *her* fault, this woman hanging over my shoulder like a vulture. If I ever had children I would baptize them all the way. No half-completed blessings, no superstitions, stigmatas, or stories. Just a life where you're like everyone else who doesn't know the answers and no one expects different.

"Hail Mary," I said as my mother squeezed my shoulder again.

February 29th was my fifteenth birthday. I was a leap baby and since it was 1988 that meant this year I had an honest-to-God birthday and I was having an honest-to-God party, except there would be no boys and my mother and aunts would chaperone. I was eating breakfast—and imagining that Jimmy would notice me for the first time as I walked past him in the school hallway, laughing with friends and trailing balloons that proclaimed "happy birthday" behind me—when my mother asked me what I was planning to wear to my party Friday evening.

My mom always acted as my alarm and then sat with me while I ate my oatmeal and she made coffee. We didn't necessarily speak to each other. Mostly we sat there, me slowly spooning oatmeal into my mouth because eating early made me queasy, and her with her chin in her hands, sometimes looking at me, sometimes getting up to check the coffee or put glasses back in the cabinet from the draining board by the sink. We always had to have the light on since the kitchen was in the center of the apartment and there was no window. The light had a dullness that made me sleepy. What also made me sleepy was the radio in the background, tuned to the news station that promised to deliver the entire world within measured increments of time. The newsman had a friendly hypnotic voice punctuated at times by a sudden rising that didn't rouse me so much as lull me further until I thought the most wonderful thing would be to drop my spoon into my bowl and put my head down on the table beside it. That morning, as the heat came up through the radiator like a bouncing Ping-Pong ball, I shrugged and answered that I didn't know what I would wear.

"Something nice, I hope?"

"I guess." It depended on your definition of nice, I thought to myself. Madonna or Heidi. Then I sneezed.

She said, "We'll go see Dr. Shapiro Saturday."

I always had a cold on my birthday and this year was no exception. It had snowed earlier in the week and whether I decided to trudge the twenty blocks to school in the snow or take the bus, my socks ended up wet. I sighed and went back to daydreaming.

By Friday, the snow had melted into a dirty gray slush, and the five girls who came to my party had so many salt crystals stuck to the bottoms of their boots that it didn't matter that they took them off in the hallway outside our door. Some of the rock salt got in anyway, and every once in a while someone cried out and tipped her foot up to remove a rock clinging to the bottom of her pantyhose.

I wore a black miniskirt. My mother disapproved but she hadn't had time to say anything since, just as I'd planned, I came out of my bedroom as the guests arrived. Actually all of the other girls wore short skirts of one type or another, except for Julie. She wore a jumpsuit with a bare back that managed to be sexier than all the miniskirts in the world.

"Hi, Mrs. C," Julie said as she handed my mom her coat.

My mother smiled thinly in response. My friendship with Julie concerned her. Though Julie was also raised by a single mother, my mother believed there to be no comparison since hers had gotten divorced.

I carried the other girls' coats to my mother's bedroom and dumped them on the bed. Nikki Castro's fell and as I bent to pick it up my mother came in with Julie's coat and said, "When you bend down I can see your whole behind."

"Don't look then." I walked down the hall to my party.

I wasn't close friends with any of these girls, except Julie, and they were more her friends than mine. We ate pizza while we played Truth or Dare. As I finished my second slice I looked around and wished my living room wasn't so strange. First there was the side table with my father's picture and the candles. Then there were the statues of saints arranged in the cabinet along the wall, all with hands raised in benediction. And to top it off there was the eight-by-ten picture of the Sacred Heart of Jesus hanging on the wall opposite the cabinet. Jesus had his hand to his exposed heart and it was burning.

We ate our pizza within this somber congress of Jesus and the

saints and I think it was this that made my guests embrace sin—
I know it often had that effect on me.

"Dare," said Rita.

Julie smiled. We all knew Rita couldn't pick Truth because of
what rumor had it may or may not have happened between her
and Bobby Jenks in the back of the bus on the class trip to Washington. Of course, I couldn't pick Truth either because I was afraid
they'd ask me what was with all the religion and why didn't I go
to dances, or what boy did I like and had I ever kissed anyone.

Julie glanced at the door to the kitchen, where my mother and
my aunts sat chatting and drinking tea. She turned back to Rita
and lowered her voice. "I dare you to act like you're having an
orgasm—a loud one, sustained for at least one minute."

The others giggled as Rita looked to the kitchen.

"Ready?" Julie asked.

Rita looked up at the picture of Jesus. "My apologies, Christ."

Julie raised her wrist to look at her watch and pointed at Rita,
who started to moan. Just loud enough. Forget the slowed-down
time I experienced during the rosaries, this had to be the longest
minute ever. A bead of sweat trickled from beneath my bra. I
attempted to blow my stuffy nose to cover the noise, but that just
made it sound as if it were ducks having sex. Finally Julie's hand
signaled stop and Rita did, after giving one last heaving cry. A
second later we heard someone's teacup meet its saucer in the
kitchen.

My mother entered the room and said it was time to open the
gifts. Her face was expressionless.

Julie's present I saved for last. I ripped the wrapping paper off the
jewelry box. Inside were gold hoops, a tiny gold hummingbird
hanging from each one; their wings were outstretched and their
beaks curved downward, as if about to drink from a flower.

"They're incredible," I said.

"Marty's ears aren't pierced," my mom said to Julie.

"They aren't?" Julie asked, laying it on a bit thick.

I had told Julie I wanted to get my ears pierced just the week before, but my mom wouldn't let me, saying only tramps had pierced ears, and Julie, who had three holes in her ear, said, "Damn straight."

"I'll get them pierced," I said, before my mother could say anything else.

Later that night, when I was getting ready for bed, my mother knocked on the bathroom door and came in. "Julie was kind enough to leave the receipt in the box."

I stopped brushing my teeth and just glared at her.

"We'll go return them after the doctor." She paused before closing the door and said, "I'm not stupid, Martina."

I spit into the sink. There was no way I was giving those earrings back.

I lay in bed that night knowing that I was damned. I used to pray before going to bed. Pray for my mother and my aunts. Pray that my father wouldn't have to spend more time in Purgatory than was necessary. Sometimes I would fall asleep praying. This was when I was little. When Purgatory was a place that I pictured daily, where my father sat on a chair reading *Life* magazine and repeatedly checking his watch, waiting to talk to me. I'd feel so guilty for falling asleep that once I punished myself by not eating. My mother saw and asked me why. When I told her, she smiled and said that that was what we were supposed to do. Fall asleep with His name on our lips. A long time had passed since I'd prayed before bed.

God would eventually have to turn away from me. Perhaps He wouldn't wait until I died to send me to Hell. He would show His disfavor while I was still on Earth, delivering unto me a horrible disfiguring disease, reversing my soul to the outside. I would contract elephantiasis of the brain. My head would swell up. Disproportionately. Not at all evenly. I would have lopsided elephantiasis of the face and it would be the mirror of my soul.

The next day I had Dr. Shapiro pierce my ears while my mother stood there and watched. She spoke only twice. "She's old enough to make her own decisions," she said when I first asked the doctor and he looked to her. And then, when he had trouble getting the hole-punching gun through my ear, she said, "That's because her head is too thick."

On the way home on the bus she removed the box with the earrings from her bag and handed it to me. She didn't speak and I forced myself not to cough or sniff, remaining as silent as she. At the stop for the pharmacy she got off the bus saying I should go home, that she would get the antibiotics for my cold.

That night we didn't say the rosary. Before my aunts could even take their coats off she said, "We're not praying."

"Why not?" Aunt Tess asked.

"Martina feels there's nothing she needs to pray for."

So we all just sat around the dinner table eating leftover birthday cake as my aunts carried on a conversation about double coupons at the A&P and my mother and I said nothing.

After my aunts left, my mother retrieved the antibiotics from her purse and then filled a glass with tap water and placed them in front of me. Then she went to bed. I stayed up a while staring at the pills and then I went to the garbage and threw them away.

Even though I'd had a doctor pierce my ears they got infected anyway. By the next day, they were red and swollen and I had a slight fever.

Briefly I thought it was my mother's curse. Over her shoulder she handed me ice to put on my ears, never saying a word, probably because she didn't have to. She'd also fished the bottle of pills out of the garbage. She'd taken one out and placed it next to a glass of water beside my oatmeal bowl. I ignored it. No matter if my ears were about to fall off, I wasn't going to give her satisfaction.

"Your mother is the most stubborn woman alive," Aunt Sylvia said.

I winced as she wiped around my ears with a cotton swab she'd dipped in rubbing alcohol. We were in my bedroom. I sat on my bed with a towel around my neck while my Aunt Sylvia stood over me and Aunt Tess leaned against the door. My mother sat in the living room watching TV.

Patting my earlobes dry with a towel, Aunt Sylvia sighed. "What she needs is a man."

"Jesus, the things that come out of your mouth," Aunt Tess said.

"Am I wrong?"

My Aunt Sylvia had never gotten married. Aunt Tess wasn't anymore. She'd been married to my Uncle Mario, who'd knocked her around before leaving her for another woman. Since their separation Aunt Tess had tried to get an annulment so she could remarry. The church's refusal had been a source of great pain to her because she felt she could not receive Communion when she was divorced and seeing another man, even though all they ever did was meet for coffee.

We heard my mother shut off the TV. No further movement could be detected from the silence. When my aunts left I stayed in my room for the rest of the night. My mother went to bed without asking how I was.

She didn't look at me for the whole week after I got my ears pierced, and sometimes I wonder if she would ever have acknowledged me again if I hadn't broken my nose. During the week, my Uncle Mario died of a heart attack, only we didn't know about it at first because he lived in Ithaca with his girlfriend and we weren't exactly "in touch."

My infection subsided but my mother continued to ignore me, handing me my dinner from the side, never completely turning. Three times a day a new pill from the bottle appeared next to the same glass of water so that by Friday night, when I entered the kitchen for dinner wearing the earrings Julie had gotten for me, there were about twenty little pink capsules all lined up on the table. My mother glanced up at me. Then she continued to scrape burnt potatoes and peppers from the bottom of a pan.

"Is that why you wanted to pierce your ears? To wear those ridiculous things?"

"Everyone wears earrings," I said, aware that I had the rebellious, self-destructive tone she was fond of censuring in others.

"Thank God, otherwise you might look stupid."

I took the plate she offered me and said, "This from a woman who wears practically the same outfit every day."

"I have had loss. What's your excuse?"

"I have a mother obsessed with something that's never going to happen."

She stopped scraping the pan and turned toward me. "Your heart is so full of bitterness and anger it's no wonder your father won't talk to you."

"My father doesn't talk to me because he's dead," I said. We stared at each other for a moment. The radio was on at a very low volume and now I faintly heard a commercial singing about gas heat. Then my mother took away the plate I still held in my hands and calmly emptied my dinner back into the pan. She slid the garbage pail over to the table, scooped up all the pills, and threw them in the garbage along with the bottle, I suppose, but I didn't know, because by then I'd gone out the door with my bike, dragged it down the stairs and out the front door.

I was so angry as I rode my bike down Ditmars that I did not experience my usual mortification at still riding a pink bike with purple sparkles on the seat. I turned at Steinway and rode until I was over the highway and I'd entered the shopping area. There were more cars here, a lot double-parked, and I needed to pay attention. It occurred to me that this was not really bike-riding weather yet, and I wasn't wearing a coat. I turned left on Broadway to escape the traffic and almost got hit by a car. It screeched to a halt. The driver slammed hard on the horn and I gave him the finger. He returned my salute and then drove on. "Asshole," I proclaimed in front of a mother and little girl who had stopped in the crosswalk to avoid getting hit by an enraged fifteen-year-old on a pink bike with purple sparkles on the seat.

It was then that the disturbing thought entered my mind. What if she was right? Maybe my father could not speak to me from heaven when my thoughts were full of hell. Which was where I was headed if I couldn't learn to be a better person, to refrain from obscenities when in the presence of innocents, to take all prescribed medications, to say "breasts" instead of "tits." It was then that I saw my Uncle Mario in a plaid suit and bow tie standing on the corner in front of Woolworth's. He crumpled up a newspaper and threw it into the trash. Unlike my great-grandmother, I immediately knew that this meant he was dead. I ran into a tree.

It was a small tree, surrounded by an inch of wire, in front of the public library. I stood up and noticed that my face was bleeding. My uncle was gone. The man from the deli came out with paper towels for my nose. Traffic had stopped for me. People who probably wished my injuries were more severe gawked at me until a police car came and took me to the emergency room. There was a moment of head-splitting agony as they reset my nose. Then the pain, though still throbbing, subsided a little. The nurse had called my mom and now she was waiting outside my room. She could come in when I was ready, the nurse told me. I wiped my tears away and braced myself for whatever her reaction would be. When I saw her face I realized she had been crying.

"I'm sorry. It's my fault," she said, embracing me.

She held me so tight that I didn't have the air to say I was sorry too.

"First the ears, and now the nose. What a klutz," my Aunt Tess said the next day.

We sat around the table eating the Chinese takeout that had just arrived. I picked up the ice pack and applied it under my right eye. Mario's girlfriend had finally condescended to call his ex-wife and Aunt Tess learned what I already knew, that Uncle Mario had died. The way was clear now for her to get guiltless coffee with her boyfriend and receive Communion.

Aunt Sylvia pulled her rosary beads out of her bag and dangled them over the table. Her eyes on my mom, she said, "Do I need these?"

My mom was silent for a moment during which I held my breath.

"No," she said, only looking at me. "I think we're done with that."

"Thank God," said Aunt Sylvia.

"It's what I was praying for that whole time," said Aunt Tess.

My mother lowered her fork in surprise. Then my Aunt Sylvia put her hand over my mother's and said, "It's what we all were praying for."

My mom smiled, then continued eating. I was still surprised she wasn't mad, but then I understood. My aunts didn't want to devote their Saturday nights to prayer either, but they did it because my mom needed to believe she'd talk to her husband again, and they loved her enough to bear with it.

I never told them what I had seen before I ran my bike into that tree. It couldn't help anything. Apparently all this gift was good for was to inform you of a death that had already happened but announce it through improper channels. Telling my mother might only have made her renew her hope and maybe even start with the rosaries again.

Although other deaths have been announced to me—for instance, a few years after Uncle Mario died I knew Sean Kirkpatrick had broken his neck playing basketball before anyone else who was not present at the actual game—just as with my uncle I never told anyone.

After my accident my mother decided to talk more about my father and I think we both preferred thinking about him alive rather than in some limbo waiting to be called forward or back. She also started wearing patterns and colors, which Aunt Tess said was a relief to her eyes. She picked vibrant shades—orange, red, and hot pink. When I visited home on breaks from college, we'd go shopping together and compete over who could find the most garish outfit.

My mother's death was a long and painful fight with cancer that she lost last year. Everyone knew she was dying and when it happened I seemed to be the only one unprepared. I keep a picture of her next to one of my father on the small table near the door in the hallway. Occasionally I'll light the candle that's there. I see my aunts every couple of months, but we only pray together twice a year—Christmas and Easter—like other modern Catholic families.

More often than not I feel I have made peace with my useless psychic ability. I still have to wait and see if, like my great-grandmother, someone, maybe my mother, will appear to me one night in the future to warn me, my husband, and my children before we are engulfed in flames.

❦ *Finalists* ❦

❧ *Omicron Ceti III* ❧

THOMAS P. BALÁZS

Three things I loved about Westchester Hospital:
1. The all-u-can-take therapy buffet.
2. The thirty-two-inch television with the Sci-Fi Channel and TV Land.
3. Rosie.

Rosie had fat cheeks and dirty-blonde hair and walked around all day long in her pajamas. She was pretty in a grown-up-mall-girl kind of way, and she had a nice rack, but that's not what made me love her. It was her quiet, gentle ways. She shuffled around the corridors of the hospital in furry slippers and flannel pee-jays, smiled at the nurses when they gave her medication, laughed at the stupidest reruns on daytime TV—*Too Close for Comfort, Full House, Saved by the Bell.* She was a soft, mellow, sleepy girl, always warm to the touch like a kitten waking up from a nap.

She sat next to me one day while I was in the lounge, flipping nonstop through channel after channel. "You need to relax," she said, and ran her palm against my forehead, smoothing down the furrows. "They're like speed bumps. You've got to slow down." She eased the remote from my hand and placed it on the coffee table in front of us.

"Close your eyes," she said, and lightly pressed my lids down with her thumb and forefinger. "Lean back." Then, she draped her arms around my waist and laid her head in my lap where seconds later she drifted off to sleep without seeming to notice there was a bump in her pillow.

Rosie slept a lot. "There's nothing in the world I like as much," she once told me. "All the things I want, I can get them in my sleep. My brother visits me, my parents leave me alone, and my baby doesn't cry. I can fly. It's like swimming, only no resistance. I breaststroke my way above the crowds, over the tops of houses. Sometimes I get too high, and then I get scared and come down, but most of the time I enjoy it. I wish I could sleep all the time and never have to wake up."

I asked her once whether she ever had nightmares, and she said, "I only have sweet dreams." That's what Rosie was for me.

You weren't supposed to date in the hospital, but, of course, people did. Rosie and I held hands on the couch when the nurses weren't looking, rubbed feet under the table at mealtimes, and always stuck up for each other in group. At night before lights out, we stood by the windows, pretending we could see the heavens through the wire mesh and the blazing white lights that illuminated the hospital.

"See that star," I would say, pointing to where I knew the night sky was. "That's Omicron Ceti III, the planet I come from."

"And there's Orion," she would say. "You know I gave him that belt."

We liked to act as though we were crazy. That way we felt superior to the others and didn't have to think about the fact that we really *were* crazy.

—

Occasions on which I have cried:

1. When Mr. Spock, in "This Side of Paradise," tells Jill Ireland he cannot love her as he once did on Omicron Ceti III.

2. When my cat Stumpy died.

3. When I thought I'd lost Rosie.

During that first occasion, I was in the arms of girlfriend number eight, who looked at me with ironic dismay.

"Are you crying? Can it be? Erik Kavanaugh actually shedding a tear?"

"Cut it out," I sniffed.

"No, really. I can't believe it. When your dad was in the hospital having part of his lung removed, you didn't cry."

"Judy, please. This is my favorite scene."

"Listen to your voice! It's squeaking! Your voice never broke the time we split up. Your voice never broke when you told me how your mother died. Your voice—"

"Jesus, Judy. Leave me alone!"

She didn't say another word, but I couldn't shut her out of my head. The whole thing was ruined, and I went as cold and silent as space itself. Later that evening we made love, mechanically as usual, except that when I came I thought about her complaint, about the *coitus interruptus* of my moment with the DVD, and the anger mounted inside me until I imagined I was shooting photon torpedoes into her uterus.

She left not long afterward.

In "This Side of Paradise," Spock goes down to Omicron Ceti III and gets sprayed by these poppy plants and spends half the show frolicking around with a young Jill Ireland. Leila, she's called. She's blonde and buxom and always in soft focus, and he's laughing and joking and hanging upside-down from trees, telling her he loves her and stuff like that. It's a beautiful thing because Spock is normally so reserved. But then the poppies wear off, and he goes back to being regular old Mr. Spock, the one who can't feel emotions. Jill Ireland tries to get him back. She says they can return to the planet, get the poppies again. But he says, "I am what I am, Leila, and, if there are self-made purgatories, we must all live in them. Mine can be no worse than someone else's."

I've watched that scene a hundred times on DVD and on the Sci-Fi Channel. I penned a letter to the writer of the episode, D.C. Fontanna, to tell her what a genius she was, but I figured she would never read it, so I just marked it, "Starship Enterprise, Star Date 3417.3," put a stamp on it, and dropped it in the mail.

"What did you hope to accomplish with that?" my therapist George asked me.

"I don't know," I said. "I just wanted to tell someone I loved their stuff."

"You loved their stuff? That's quite an admission from you, Erik."

"What? I love that episode. I can't love something? I'm a robot?"

"Those are your words, not mine."

Actually they weren't mine either. They were Diane's, girlfriend number six. She once compared me to Data, the android from *Star Trek: The Next Generation.* "It's like you've got no feelings at all, like Data—only at least he tries."

I resented the remark. I hate *The Next Generation.* Data is a pale imitation of Spock, a mere Pinocchio retread. I told her as much while she was walking out the door.

Three theories for why I am the way I am:

1. Freudian: My mother died in a car crash when I was fourteen, just as I was emerging from sexual latency, overwhelming

me with Oedipal guilt and cutting off access to the libido, leading to a general lack of affect punctuated by occasional eruptions from the unconscious.

2. Jungian: My father's emotional abandonment of me following the accident left me with a gaping "father wound," hemorrhaging vitality and preventing me from mourning the loss of both parents.

3. Spockian: See above section on self-made purgatories.

Rosie loved me just the way I was.

"I'm no lover boy," I once told her, echoing Warren Beatty's speech to Faye Dunaway in *Bonnie and Clyde*. He tells her that right after they've robbed their first bank, and she gets so worked up she starts smothering him with kisses while he's driving the getaway car. In my case, Rosie and I had just snatched a smooch while the other refugees from reality lined up for meds. "I mean, I'm not impotent or anything—not physically, anyway. Emotionally, though, I have trouble getting it up."

"You'll just have to use your tongue then," she laughed. "Tell me what you know you should feel."

Talk about taking lemons and making lemonade; this girl could make tuna casserole from kitty litter. That's why I never understood why she had so much trouble taking care of herself and her baby.

"I can't look at him without wanting to go to sleep," she told me. "Even when my parents bring him here to see me it's all I can do to stay awake."

"Postpartum depression?"

"Post-party depression," she said. "I knew I shouldn't have joined that game of beer die. I should sue Pabst Blue Ribbon for child support."

Beer die was a college drinking game. It was like Quarters, only you used dice and a wooden board, not unlike a knock-hockey board. Suing the beer manufacturer probably would have been her best bet, considering that, short of paternity tests, she had no way of knowing which of the five guys she'd slept with that night bounced his sperm successfully into the cup of her womb.

In Westchester Hospital, however, paternity was mostly irrelevant. We rarely had enough time together alone to share more than a brief kiss. Still, those kisses were never rushed. Rosie's mouth would open to mine as if in a yawn, and her tongue nosed around my mouth like a tired, wet otter exploring a hidden cave.

The hospital, like our kisses, was outside of time. Sure, there was a kind of chronology: Meals at seven, twelve, and five. Meds at nine and three. Group therapy at one. Individual therapy at eleven. But all those things were just like railings on a path that stretched forever before and behind you. There were no mile markers, no days of the week, not even months. We were both in there for the long-term. Rosie couldn't keep a job, barely fed herself, much less her baby, and had overdosed on sleeping pills in the hope of inducing a coma and dreaming forever. And me, I couldn't stop talking in threes.

Three things I loved about Stumpy:

1. He was a one-man cat. Stumpy couldn't give a damn about the rest of the world. When people came over and tried to pet him, he'd shy away or lick the place they'd touched as if their fingers were covered with excrement. Then he'd come up to me, rub against my leg, and leap onto my lap. Jane, girlfriend number nine, said the cat was in love with me.

2. He thought he was a dog. He would fetch, roughhouse, and sleep on the bed. One woman, who was around too short a time to be counted, objected to him napping there. It was her or him. It was him.

3. He never asked me for anything I couldn't give.

It wasn't long after Judy left me for good that I got Stumpy. I had never seen a cat without a tail before, and unlike all the other mewing kittens at the pound, he pretty much ignored me. Apparently he was a Manx, but they couldn't say for sure. Sometimes things like that just happen, they said. I poked his little Beanie-Baby body, and he raised his head, glared at me, and went back to sleep. The perfect cat, I thought. I could use some companionship, but not too much. I had talked to my then-current therapist—I forget his name—about getting on antidepressants. I had become a regular visitor to the back room of Video Express, and now I would have a cat. Pussycat, Prozac, and pornography. That's all I needed.

My dad was visiting my apartment in Chelsea. He wanted to see where I lived, what I was doing, whether I was taking care of my teeth. He took me out to dinner, told me stories about my mother, how he had never loved anyone like he had loved her, how when she died and left him alone, he didn't think he'd be able to cope, how he threw himself even more into his practice because he knew the one thing he could do was to support me financially. I didn't know what he was getting at. Some kind of grand apology. Apparently he'd just met some new woman, and it was like the spring thaw of his heart, and he wanted me to meet her, and even though I was all grown up now, he wanted my approval. Whatever. I approved.

Back in my apartment, he threw open the window and leaned out over Sixth Avenue.

"New York is some kind of place. Are you happy here?"

I said I was.

That's when Stumpy leapt onto the windowsill, and my dad tried to pet him, and the cat took a swat at my dad and lost his footing. Some people think cats need a tail for balance. Others say that's a myth. In Stumpy's case, it's hard to know. Maybe if he'd had a tail, he wouldn't have fallen off the ledge. Then again, maybe if it hadn't been for the fire hydrant between him and the sidewalk, he would have landed on his feet. He died in the taxi on the way to the animal hospital, and I wept all the way to Bellevue.

Therapists loved me. Frank, my first shrink, was head over heels.

"It's so tragic," he would say. "Your mom and your dad on their way to see you in a junior high school melodrama in which you play the villain; the icy road, the three-car pileup, your dad trapped in there with her as she dies, the jaws of life…"

"Jaws of death I'd say."

"They got *him* out."

"In a matter of speaking."

I saw Frank once a week for nearly three years in high school, during which time he educated me in the ways of Viennese Voodoo. He claimed I was stuck on my mother, had not had the chance to renounce my erotic attachment to her before she got killed, and that I blamed both my father and myself for her death.

"In your unconscious fantasies, you imagine it was your desire for her that resulted in the accident. It's a reverse Oedipus. I mean it's classic. She was even killed at a three-way intersection! So you figure you killed your mother, and now you're left alone with your father who is the one person you really wanted out of the way. No wonder you can't feel."

I always had trouble with that whole erotic-attachment-to-my-mother business. How can you be Oedipally attached to someone you never see? I didn't even know they'd been on the way to the play. They never came to my school stuff.

But Frank had another theory. I had not only lost my mother but also my father in that accident. Neither of us could face the other afterward. So Frank was going to be substitute mama *and* papa for me. "A corrective emotional experience," he called it. He was going to pick up where they had left off. So, he would ask me about swim team and how I had done, get on my case if I didn't do my homework, encourage me to go back to acting. When I broke 1300 on the SATs, he slapped my back and yelped for joy. He and his wife even came to my high school graduation. I guess they had a lot of time; they had no kids of their own.

The day before I went off to college, Frank went to pieces. When he opened the door onto our last session, his eyes were bloodshot. His hair—what there was of it—was a mess. He must have spent the night in the office. He gestured toward the couch and sobbed something about countertransference.

The guy at Bellevue was less analytical.

"Oedipus schmedipus," he said. "Let's try adding Wellbutrin to the Prozac."

"Sure. Could you prescribe a low-milligram dose of potassium cyanide as well?"

"Maybe we better keep you in here for a few days."

They loved me.

My dad said he loved me, kept saying it over and over again, *ad nauseum,* in the cab, first on the way to the animal hospital while I clutched my bleeding kitty in my arms and wailed like the mother of Christ, then on the way to the lunatic hospital while I accused him of having the touch of death.

"You're a modern-day Midas. Everything you touch turns to shit. How do your patients survive your fingers in their mouths? Why don't their teeth turn to turds? Oh that's right, you wear gloves. That probably helps. You should wear them all the time. You should wear a full-fucking body suit."

"Erik," he said, "Erik, I'm sorry. I love you. It wasn't my fault. He just jumped away. I just came here to see how you were doing, to try and straighten things out."

Never trust an orthodontist to straighten things out. That's what I was thinking, but I couldn't speak anymore. I was trying not to heave my brunch all over the back of the cab.

Other movie, television, and theatrical characters with whom I identify:

1. Bogart in *Casablanca*. I mean the part at the end, not during those cheesy flashbacks in Paris, but the part where he's telling Ingrid Bergman to get on the plane, and he's looking all cool in his trench coat and fedora.

2. Eastwood in *High Plains Drifter*. He just rides into town out of nowhere, casually rapes a woman in a barn, kills a few people, spits tobacco. Never cracks a smile or blinks or says he's sorry.

3. Judas Iscariot in *Jesus Christ Superstar*. I don't know why I like this guy because he's one tortured individual, and he doesn't even get to mess around with Mary Magdalene. But when he sings the reprise of *I Don't Know How to Love Him*, I feel like it's me on that CD. Though, let me say for the record that it is *only* Murray Head, the Judas from the original brown and yellow soundtrack, who does anything for me. The rest of the Judases, Ben Vereen included, don't know Judas from a hole in the hand.

My parents and I went to see *J. C. Superstar* back in 1977, when I was six years old and it was revived on Broadway. But I suppose that's overstating the case. My mother misremembered the time on the tickets, and we arrived an hour late and were not let into the first act. My father threw a tantrum, said the best music was in the first half of the show, and he was going for a walk and would meet us afterward.

"A walk? A walk where?" my mother asked. It was starting to snow.

"A walk," is all he said.

She and I hung around in the lobby under the watchful eyes of the ushers for the next half-hour, my mother biting her lower lip as she often did when she was angry. Then the two of us went in for the second act, which is, in fact, far superior to the first with its woe-is-me whining and sloppy sentimentality. Really, the final half of the show not only features the Judas rendition of *I Don't Know How to Love Him,* but also Herod's taunting of Jesus and Pilate's execution of the thirty-nine lashes. My dad was seriously misinformed. Anyway, afterward, my mom and I sat in a coffee shop to await his return from wherever he had gone. We left a note on the car windshield telling him where we were, but it was soon covered over in snow. It took him a good while to figure that out, so our stay in the coffee shop was far longer than we spent at the Longacre Theatre. Yeah, he was crazy in love, that dad of mine.

I would have waited an age in Hell for Rosie if we were late getting to see Jesus. The problem was Rosie got ahead of me.

Three reasons Rosie and I couldn't stay together in the psyche-sanctuary for all eternity:
  1. Someday Westchester Hospital would cease to exist.
  2. Someday Rosie and I would cease to exist.
  3. Insurance wouldn't cover it.
  "Do you know you compulsively make lists of three?" a girl in group once asked me. "Three movies I'd like to see, three things I'd like for dinner, 'my three favorite selective serotonin reuptake inhibitors."
  "Three's a sacred number. The Father, the Son, the Holy Ghost. The past, the present, and the future. The ego, the id, and the super ego."
  "It's weird."
  "The Three Little Pigs, Goldilocks and the Three Bears, the Three Stooges."
  "Okay. I get the point."

"*My Three Sons. Three's Company. Three to be You and Me.*"

"That's Free *to be You and Me.*"

"Once, twice, three times a lady. Rub-a-dub-dub, three men in a tub. I'm as three as a bird."

"*Free*bird! It's *Free*bird."

"Free, three, what's the difference?"

"That's an interesting question," said Jonathan, one of the group facilitators. "Can you be free of three?"

"Oh please," I said. "Don't get Freudian on me. Or Jungian. Or Adlerian."

It began when I emerged from my crying jag over Stumpy and continued right on through Bellevue and Westchester Hospital. All day long, everything in threes.

At dinner, "I'll have peas, broccoli, and carrots."

"We don't have broccoli."

"I'll have peas, carrots, and potatoes."

"We don't have potatoes."

"I'll have peas, carrots, and peas!"

During visiting hours, "I don't want to see my father. I don't want to see my mother. I don't want to see anyone."

"Your mother's not here."

"That's because she's dead, dead, dead."

With George during our sessions, "So why this obsession with three?"

"First, I don't agree it's an obsession. Second, I happen to like the number. Third, get off of my case."

But Rosie didn't care; she was able to use it, to channel it, to sublimate it, if you will.

"Tell me three things you love about me," she would say.

"I love your sweet eyes, your soft lips, and your warm, flannel-covered breasts."

"So you only love me for my body?"

"I love the way you kiss me, the touch of your hands, the sound of my name on your lips."

"So you only love me for what I do for you?"

"I love the way you eat, the way you sleep. I love everything about you."

Like I said, I was never much of a lover boy, but with Rosie, it was easy.

It seemed like a long, lazy eon before my father was there, telling me I could leave soon. "Dr. Gregory says the suicidal ideation has subsided, and you're getting the counting thing under control."

"Do you know you're the third person who's told me I'm ready to leave? You, Dr. Gregory, the head nurse."

"Everyone thinks you're improving."

"I don't think I am. Rosie doesn't think I am. The other people in the group don't think I am."

"Blue Cross and Blue Shield thinks you are," he said, trumping my girlfriend, my peers, and me.

Rosie and I began to plot ways of proving I was unfit for society.

"You could weep uncontrollably again," she said.

"I can't cry on command. I usually can't cry at all."

"You could play with yourself in group."

"In front of John and Karen? No way."

"You could make a suicidal gesture."

"I might succeed."

Then a strange thing happened. Rosie got out first.

It was my fault. As I started to get better, I developed a kind of Stockholm Syndrome, identification with the oppressors, like Patty Hearst, and I started practicing lay therapy.

"Have you had your thyroid checked?" I asked Rosie.

"God, what haven't I had checked? Yes, I think so. They said it was normal."

"You know those tests can be wrong sometimes. I think you should get it checked again. You've got all the classic symptoms of hormonal deficiency. You're a little young for it, but still, it often happens after pregnancy."

"I thought you majored in sociology?"

"I did, but my mother was a psychiatrist."

She let out a big yawn. *Taxi* was just starting on TV Land, so we let the subject drop, but she spoke to her parents about it, and they spoke to the doctors, and they ran the tests again, and, sure enough, I was right. They started her on the hormone treatment, and a few weeks later, the doctors decided she could do a halfway kind of thing, come in for just the day, do group and individual therapy, get her meds administered, have lunch, and then go home at night.

She didn't want to leave. Yet, as she stood in the corridor with her suitcase, her hazel eyes already sparkled with new life. Dressed in gray and blue, she withdrew from sight like a cloud floating away.

My eyes were sparkling too, but not with life. I didn't get as bad as I did over Stumpy, but it was worse than my reaction to when Spock dumps Leila, and one of the nurses actually put her paw on my shoulder to comfort me.

Things weren't the same at Westchester without Rosie. In the evenings, I lingered by the window, staring out into the night, but all I could see was the glare. I tried to make things more interesting in group by challenging John and Karen's facile interpretations, but that just annoyed everyone.

"I liked you better when you were talking in threes," said the girl who only a few months ago had been driven to distraction by my triads.

"I never liked you much, period," I said. I was getting back to my old self.

Shortly thereafter, they put me on the part-time plan too, and I went to go live with my dad and stepmom-to-be. They hadn't gotten married yet, and technically, they weren't living together, but she was there all the time. She was okay, really. Nothing like my mother. She was a businesswoman, worked in orthodontic administration recruiting interior mouth decorators for various medical systems. She dressed in blue suits and wore her hair up and used a lot of makeup and always wore earrings. She was handsome rather than pretty and teased my father in ways I don't ever remember my mother doing.

"I'm teaching John to play golf," she said one night at dinner. "We have to pay an extra green fee for all the divots he leaves."

Golf. The clubs my mother bought my father one Christmas gathered dust in the basement for twenty years. Heather fished them out to get him started, but then decided they were obsolete and bought him a whole new set. He was playing tennis too, and they were taking weekend trips to the Catskills and to little bed and breakfasts in Connecticut. They even went and caught the second revival of *J.C. Superstar* on Broadway. Heather got them there early.

I wasn't doing much myself. I spent my days in sweats and t-shirts, not even bothering to put on jeans when I went to the hospital for the day program, and when I got home I slept and watched TV.

I didn't see Rosie anymore. They had, apparently, assigned us to different groups. So one night I called her.

"Hey," she said. "You escaped."

"More like dragged out."

"Still talking in threes?"

"No," I said. "George has me writing down lists instead. It seems to help."

There was something odd about her voice. I couldn't quite place it at first. I thought maybe she was uncomfortable talking to me because of where we had met.

"You sound different." It was energy, I realized. She was awake.

"It's the hormone therapy, just like you said. It's made all the difference. Can you believe I'm taking care of the baby all by myself now? Well, almost all by myself. My mom watches him when I take night classes."

"Night classes?"

"Yes, I'm finishing my degree."

"Terrific," I said. "Great."

She asked me if I wanted to come over and see the baby. I told her no thanks. I was busy.

"Busy doing what?"

"Sleeping," I said. "I've been doing lots of sleeping."

At the end of "This Side of Paradise," Kirk and McCoy discuss their experience on the planet. McCoy says that once again man has been thrown out of paradise, and Kirk says, no, this time we walked out on our own, and he makes a big pompous speech about marching to the sound of drums. Then he turns to Spock.

"You haven't said what you thought about Omicron Ceti III."

"I don't have much to say about it," Spock responds, "except that for the first time in my life I was happy." Cut to the credits.

"You are not Spock," George told me.

"That's just what Leonard Nimoy said. 'I am not Spock.' And then he went and did half a dozen sequels."

"How many sequels do you hope to do at Westchester?"

Then one day, Rosie showed up on my doorstep when my dad and Heather just happened to be out. She was smiling broadly in jeans and a t-shirt that nicely showed off her pillowy breasts, and her beer-die prize was in the crook of her arm, perched on her hip.

"It's the welcome wagon."

"I'd prefer the paddy wagon." But I let her and the offspring in.

He was okay, that kid. I mean, he was no Stumpy. He didn't fetch or roughhouse or anything, but he crawled around a lot. His balance wasn't much better than my old cat's. He would try and stand up every once in a while, only to topple over. But he didn't cry much, and I liked that. Jimmy was his name.

That first night, we just sat and watched the toddler tumble, and we didn't touch or kiss or anything even though it was the first time we had ever really been alone. Then Rosie began stopping by every Monday evening until one time when she came in the middle of the week. She was on her way to school, but she had the baby with her.

"My parents couldn't watch him, and I don't want to take him to class."

Talk about setups.

"You're going to leave him here with me? Are you kidding? Did you bring his litter box?"

She was not kidding, and she had brought his diapers, which she showed me how to use. "You're a smart guy. You can handle it."

When she left, I sat my charge down next to me and popped *Star Trek* Volume 17 into the DVD player to watch "This Side of Paradise" one more time, but Jimmy would not pay attention. He kept crawling off the couch and tugging on my arms, and he did need to be changed—not once, not twice, but thrice.

Thus, I became the kid's weekly Wednesday sitter. It was the only job I had for months, and I was pretty good at it. We'd watch TV, and I'd bounce him on my knee and try to teach him tricks like chasing a ball of aluminum foil, all the while thinking of those sleeping pills Rosie had taken and how she had failed in her attempt to rid herself of daily woes. Maybe, I thought, it's because suicide is a man's job. George once said that women tried more often to take own their lives, but men had a higher success rate. And the thought stuck with me for a long time, to go boldly where so many men have gone before.

Finally, I sat down with half a gallon of orange juice and a tremendous bottle of fluoride tablets I'd obtained with a prescription pad heisted from my dad's office. I had read online that you could OD on the stuff if you took enough, and it seemed appropriate to whack myself with a dental wonder drug. Vicodin, Codeine, those were so pedestrian. I wanted a suicide with a measure of poetic justice. Somewhere, I thought, there was a six-foot cavity in the ground waiting to be filled. Of course, my father was an orthodontist, so it was kind of a stretch, as suicidal metaphors go.

At any rate, I hadn't yet decided whether to swallow the huge chalky tablets whole or to crush them into the juice. Either way, I'd have to get down quite a few to do the job. While I was thinking it over, I took out the pencil and pad I had been carrying in my shirt pocket since coming home and started to write a list of three reasons why I should still go on living.

I only came up with two: Rosie and Jimmy.

❧ *Sundress* ☙

ARIANA-SOPHIA KARTSONIS

Grandmama called Winter the season of white flies. I don't know why I remember this now, but I do when I'm walking and flakes fly at my cheeks, my eyes and the sky is white, menacing—I think of a swarm of snow buzzing and whirling.

Things in my grandmother's world are hostile, crazed, attacking. She's been committed to the insane asylum seven times since I was born. Grandmama shrieks at the windows like a trapped bird.

"They circle the house," she'd whisper to me, "they are gathering the widows now, they are taking us away."

"Hush," my father would say, "hush now."

"All the widows in the city, widows and orphans, you better watch out too little Missy," one bedpost-finger stabbing towards me, "you're a little half-orphan girl, widows and orphans, they want us all."

I cried when she called me an orphan, half because she scared me, half because it felt so true.

"That will be enough for tonight, Old Woman, enough already," and something in his tone would quiet her for a while. Though she'd sit in the corner, wild-eyed, resigned as if she knew what we were so tragically unaware of, and she'd leave us to our hideous fates if we wouldn't hear her warnings.

She left when I was five and a half. Middle of my kindergarten year. By first grade, I learned: girls without mamas look different somehow, smell different, their crooked ribbons wilt, fray from the edges, hang longer on the right side than the left. Even back then and so young, other girls knew you were different, smelled it on you the way animals can smell a wound on one another a good mile back. Other little girls couldn't always name it, but they felt it coming off you like a haunting and they kept their distance.

My mother's name is Layla.

"Like the night," my daddy said. "Your mother's name means darkness in Arabic."

Layla. The sweet word that wove in and out of us like perfume hands on cartoons, fast and stopped in place at the same time. Scarves and hummingbirds and heartbeat, Layla: a word that lived in parts apart, ragged scraps that I tried to sew together to get *mother*, but there were big spaces left behind. So this is what we have of her: seams on the backs of stockings, white embroidery on my pillowcase, an old bottle of sticky nailpolish, plus Layla, a sound hard on my daddy's ears, nice on mine. Not *mama* like my babydoll says when you tip her back and rock her forward, just Layla like Clapton's song, the slow version, *Layla, you got me on my knees, Layla.*

I used to wonder about her, what it would be like to have her saying soft things when I needed to hear them. *It's okay Angel-Puss*, she'd say into my hair when I fell down, like the little boy next door's mama said when he skinned his knee: *You're just fine, Little Heart, just fine.*

I collect names of places that sound pretty to me, *Eau Claire, Coeur d'Alene, Telluride.* "Someday," I'd tell my pretend sister, "I'm going everywhere."

I harbored a secret crush on Steven Harris, a boy with hair like spun gold and burnished bronze, his brassy, ruddy complexion and baby blue eyes. Something about the way his lashes touched his cheeks when he looked down for kick-the-can or up to bat when he spit once at the dirt by his feet then glanced up, squinted at the sun, but not before those lashes brushed his cheeks full-on, just once—I could feel it clear back in the outfield.

The men in town say things about my father.

"Our tax dollars go to buy that cripple all the sweet wine he can drink."

The government gives my daddy bunches of money, more, he tells me, then he'd get if he was a doctor or a lawyer. My daddy said to ask those men how much they'd sell their legs for and my daddy, he'd buy them. My daddy stepped smack into a land mine, "left my legs hanging there like rope licorice."

The men in town tell me: "Your daddy can get a desk job, at the post office or the bank, the only thing wrong with the rest of him is that nasty thirst of his. Your daddy could make some use of himself, give something back."

My daddy gave his legs, I wanted to tell the men at the barbershop. I think that's something—I think that's something else.

People say my mama made a fool of him, took off eight years later with some big rancher from San Antone.

Now my daddy doesn't want to talk about it.

"Beautiful woman," is all he'll ever say. "Beautiful like the night."

Sandusky, Abilene, Aberdeen, St. Cloud.

The difference between a town and a city is how few words it takes to sum you up for the people that live there. I'm the girl whose mama left home for a *real man.* I'm the girl whose pa's in a wheelchair. *In a wheelchair*, as if it could say everything about him, kept there inside the wheelchair: a giant tortoise-man connected from the inside to the chair. A reptilian body in a turtle shell, as if we could just cut into the drab green vinyl and find him there: soul and spirit.

From the pity-faces I was given when I'd push my father into the barbershop or to the newsstand, I knew before I could articulate it, that the disabled were a species to themselves—as if there had never been a pa before this one—so connected to what he was not. As if he'd been born this way, a legless infant rolling out of his mother in a miniature wheelchair into the doctor's hands. A sugarsnap pea grown into the pod that contained him.

On the side of our house is a flight of cracking concrete stairs leading to a basement we rent out to Raphael and Raoul. A parrot called Medallin squawks from the downstairs apartment. No one ever taught him to talk so he just makes noises.

"Like you," Raphael says, "the mute senorita, that bird don't talk."

Raphael talks soft to me and when he talks, he looks down like he's shy. His skin and hair and eyes are dark and so rich they remind me of chocolate ice cream on brownies with hot fudge sauce. Sometimes coming back from the market, I'd take two dollars out of my pa's change and stop at the drugstore for chocolate, chocolate-chip ice cream with chocolate syrup.

"Don't know how you do that, girl," the man would say, spooning the second scoop into my plate, finishing with a drizzle of sauce. "This much chocolate would make me crazy."

Afterwards when it was so hot, the most punitive part of summer, I'd go home and fall asleep on the couch and dream strange, burnt-edged, scorched sugar dreams. When Raphael looked up for just a flash, a bashful grin in his eyes, I felt that same sugary stupor like too much dessert.

Raoul gives me the creeps, his quiet voice always sounds like it's making fun of you or making a joke that only he understands. Raoul looks straight into your eyes, then down your body then back up at your face with his funny little smile. If Raphael is there, he sometimes says: "Leave the little girl alone, Raoul, let's go."

At Bless the Beasts pet store the parrot is all blue and green and it says "Hey Little Lady," or "Cry me a river, I'll sing you a song." Sometimes he just says "I don't want your stupid cracker, Polleeeeeeee."

I go there a lot when I don't want to be home but not to see the parrot. I go to see my bird, a cockatiel, all white with a cradle moon over her eyes.

Sometimes I go there after school to see her, pillow-white and soft as cloud. When I walk in the door the parrot says: "Penny for your thoughts. Penny for your thoughts."

I read all the books there: the fish ones, the birds, the different breeds of dogs and cats. I even read the one about the parrot insane asylum in Australia. It said parrots are so sensitive to companionship, that when neglected they sink into a kind of depression, pound their heads against their cages, pluck out their feathers with their beaks, break their own wings. The book said a mad parrot can only dip so far into sadness before no matter how much attention the bird is given, it is too far gone.

I want to go to those parrots, the ones left in cages until they're mad from sadness and I want to open each of their little doors and send them on their way.

Meridian, Santa Clara, Paradise.

One night—late—Raoul came upstairs when my father had fallen asleep, bottle in his hand.

"Your old man here?" he said, from the wrong side of the screen door startling me while I stood at the sink doing dishes.

"He's sleeping," I said, gesturing to the living room.

"You look startled, like a doe," he said, "you think I'm a hunter?"

"I didn't hear you come in." I said turning back to the sink, conscious of the thin cotton of my t-shirt. I thought he was turning to go when I felt him brush his rough cheek against my arm, then his hand on my belly.

"Hush," he said, "hush" and I ran like the ssshhh of that word was a bullet. I sidestepped him from the sink and exploded through the screen door. I ran down the street, all the way to the pet store with its one light on in the back and the quiet birds and covered cages and the new kittens in the window curled into little furry donuts. I stood there most of the rest of the night watching the animals sleep.

"Bone-secrets of the moon," my daddy called them. Those things you whisper deep in prayers, the moon hears and keeps safe, deep-nested, way down in the sweet dark marrow of her bones. I thought that's where their dreams were kept, animals and insects, even the high-ether dreams of birds on the wing, in the cachet-center of the moon. I imagined the moon as a jar of face cream like the one that said *night cream* that my mother left behind, the kind that when you twisted off the metal lid released a smell of milk and muffled flowers.

My daddy said wonderful things sometimes, even when I knew he was drunk, I loved the scratchy sound of his voice, the way the words leaned into each other as if they were tired but also patient. During the ping-ping-ping of hailstorms, he'd roll up to the window and stare out at the dotted-swiss of our yard.

"Pillstorm," he'd say to that kind of weather.

On school mornings, I'd leave him there, and walk outdoors into my daddy's idea of a world as a flurry of aspirin, a giant's worn wool sweater, pilled-up and dropped over our reduced, snowglobe-sized life.

—

I was sent home one Thursday in fifth grade when a group of kids tore the legs off a daddy long leg just to watch the helpless dust-colored dot sit there, alive and tortured.

"What about that, you creepy, crippled bug? You're no daddy long leg now."

"You're a daddy no leg," Lenny Green said.

"I know whose daddy that is," Steven Harris said and gave me a sneer.

Something in me broke, all that silence just shattered and I stood in the middle of the playground and screamed until it felt like little slivers of spun glass, little bits of angel hair lined my throat, until I felt like my lungs were bleeding and still the sound came.

By junior high I started hanging out with Sunny Dorin who'd gone grocery shopping with her mother the summer of sixth grade and was waiting in the truck while her mother loaded the two bags of groceries into the bed. Sunny accidentally put the truck into gear then panicked. The truck took her mother off guard, knocked her underneath, crushed her beneath it. She was pressed that way a good fifteen minutes before the ambulance came, loaded her mother on the stretcher covered her up, face and all, with the sheet, and sedated Sunny.

Sunny had been all her name implied before, shiny, popular, perfect, and if you'd asked anyone: the happiest girl in school. But by the time she came back from summer vacation, she was different, a damaged girl with smelly hair, and me, lonely as I was, I was morbid enough to think, maybe I'll have a friend finally. Sunny wouldn't talk for the longest time and aside from the taunting from some of the boys *Sunny Dorin took an ax, gave her mother forty whacks...* hardly anyone talked to her either.

It took a long time, a long, long time and I'd known it would and couldn't possibly care less if it did, months later I'd still be lonely, at least with Sunny I had a project and a chance to have a first friend. This Sunny was like a new, doomed girl moving in, nothing like the girl I'd watched every year at school with her perfect clothes and hair, but like a tough girl from another city. This new Sunny wore only dark, rumpled clothes, smoked clove cigarettes, seemed older, much older than the old Sunny. Sunny's problem was different from mine, but the same in the way other little girls stood clear of her as if death were contagious—or death could be less contagious than it is. They might catch your dead mama the way they'd catch a cold or just *dead* that mysterious, sickly idea that hung off you like the wrong label on designer jeans.

"Want one?" she said, offering me a cigarette, her first words to me and I took it, even though I'd never smoked before, I took that first gift.

"They taste good," I said licking over the sweetness of my lips with the first spicy breath.

"Make your lungs bleed," Sunny said in a flat voice, "I like them."

I was careful for a long time not to talk about death or mothers or trucks. Sunny talked about death all the time, loved gruesome stories from the news.

"What do you want to be when you die?" she'd say, then blow a smoke ring and look off at nothing in particular.

This Sunny, the damaged girl with hair so oily sometimes that I could still see the comb tracks when it had been combed at all, was half-mean, and cautious as dumpster cats. But I didn't mind, like I didn't mind hand-me-down clothes from the church bin when I could get them or the leftover rolls off the cafeteria trays when I had lunch duty. I was used to the next-to-last thing, the make-do, the half-used-up, and if Sunny Dorin had moved on and a new girl who loved dying moved in and I could have a friend, even a fractured friend, I wasn't proud, I could get by. In my mind I called this new girl *Sonny Despair*—a child of misery like me.

My other life was another story. My make-believe sister was amazing, with glossy lips and shampoo-ad hair. My pretend sister and I needed two closets each for our prom dresses and shoes lined up on the floor as if an army of ghost women stood upright with their glass-clear feet in neat pairs all through our wardrobes.

My mother named me Winter Clara. She still loved my father back then and they had gone to the Nutcracker ballet and she sat on his lap in the chair and my father scooted them both along with his strong arms. I've seen the old photographs how they used to dance like that: daddy in his chair and mama with her arms looped around him, facing him, craning her neck back, her hair falling back, away from her body like a waterfall.

My daddy was raised poor as poor and when the check came every month, he put most of it into savings. I know, because he called me in after school the first of the month to cash it at the Sam's SouperMarket, then run down to the night box at the bank and deposit all but the little bit we use to buy our groceries and pay our bills. My daddy didn't mean to keep me looking all faded and poor, he just didn't think about fresh dresses and brand new denims I could wear into soft blue that Sunny Dorin's jeans had to them. I hadn't had nice panties since the ones with the days of the week embroidered in a little scalloped edge circle on the back-side. But I didn't know how to ask my daddy for those things, so I wore them until just Thursday and Sunday were left without holes in them and the elastic pinched so that I could hardly stand it. My mama used to buy pretty dresses with the money some-times, I'd guess, because she left some of them behind but my daddy wanted to save that money. So I learned to take a little from the grocery money each time, stash it away to buy napkins and new underpants. Then back through town where the men— I was sure—seemed to sneer at my secret.

Passing Bob's Barbershop I heard them once as I walked away.

"That man, makes his girl live in near poverty so he can guzzle the grape juice. You seen the way his daughter is dressed?"

Because girls without mamas, are also, I guess, part-deaf.

My pa could hit the bottle pretty hard. Saturday, two o'clock in the morning and I have the keys to the truck biting into the heel of my right hand. I find him on Front Street, the main road cutting through town, popping wheelies in his chair, leaning way back and teetering on its big wheels, the silver spokes like batons of light spinning in the dark. He's alone and laughing , bottle in hand, turning figure eights. I kill the lights, wait in the truck for him to tip the chair, he will and it won't be long. When I go to him he says, "That you, Winter-girl? You look just like your mama, sometimes."

I lift the chair with the help of my father's strong arms pushing back on the ground,

"Winter-girl," he says, "coming to your pa's rescue again."

I couldn't bring myself to remind him it was my fifteenth birthday. Instead, I turned up the radio while he slumped against the passenger window, the lights glittering his wet eyes as we drove home to the sound of a gospel preacher: "Who ya gonna call when your soul's in trouble? The sinbuster Hisself—God Almighty!"

I learned to drive when I turned twelve and by now the road from his favorite drinking holes and back seemed to reel the car up like black ribbon—slack and running right up to our front door.

—

These are the dreams from the old house, crabapple tree catching me in the web of shadow branches as they fall across my bed. I'd lie in my usual spider-silence and begin to slip into dreams: our faucet runs water sapphires, runs them into my hands, through my fingers, clogs our drain, spills out of the sink onto the floor, until our kitchen floods with them. At first I'm happy, wearing robes and coats with deep pockets and filling them, finding pails to pour all those glassy jewels into. In the dream my heart races imagining bringing the stones to my father. At first, I love all the stones raining into our house, then I realize I'm thirsty and now we have nothing to drink. The men from town start saying *all the sweet wine he can drink* and my daddy says *how much for your legs?* to the men in town and then I hear water running in the bathroom next to my room. These are the dreams that I had when I was twelve and a half.

I could save a hundred pennies in two weeks, finding them on the sidewalks or back in change when Daddy sent me for groceries. When I had a hundred, I'd head over to the Olde Apothecary and buy a horehound sucker with the wooden stick, eight jawbreakers with their tart, colorful secret centers—chalky as I imagined the bone-secrets of the moon must be—I also bought five Swedish raspberries and a candy lipstick for my pretend sister.

I called it my secret center because I didn't know of another word that wasn't dirty like Raoul would've called it or babytalk like private or thingy. When I wiped there was a brightness, a shocking red, like cranberry juice, a brilliant plume of blood on the tissue.

"Sunny, I think I'm dying." Dying always got Sunny's attention, so I tried to explain.

"Off-floor, you know like in gym class," Sunny kept saying, but I didn't know, I heard *eau fleur*, some French phrase that meant nothing for me, some strange phrase our gym teacher said we should say if we couldn't swim that day. It was two weeks later, to the day when we studied menstruation in health class, when they divided the boys from the girls. The other girls complained but I was entranced by the little flower-shaped tubes they called fallopian with their petal fingers holding on to the soft eggs. I was mesmerized by what a body could know without a mother to explain.

My body had been changing, I made a makeshift brassiere from one of my father's tee-shirts cut to a long rectangular rag and tied so tight around my breasts, it was as if I wanted to suffocate them away. I knew what a bra was but couldn't stand the pitiful look of the salesclerk in the budding beauties section of J.C. Penney's, couldn't bear the touch of one more sympathetic woman's hands smoothing over me with a saccharine pitying tenderness for the girl without a mama, measuring a girl like that…

My body had changed, even without my mama's words to tell me what it meant, my candy pink nipples had lost their opacity, had grown from nickels to fifty-cent pieces in diameter and the stretch had lent a kind of translucence as if now the nipples were made up of spills of clear pink water on the breasts, the pale domes coming through that pink sheerness, as if they were just swirls from my mama's clear pink rose-water blush, a glass bottle full of tired pink liquid that leaves color on the skin, a gauzy, filmy color suspended on the surface like pink tears. My body had been changing but I didn't know to expect a culmination, a finale of blood like an opera or a bad western.

In the dream it is always early morning, and my father is a black cutout against a creepy purple blue-black sky. His silhouette is slouched and sorry. Water sapphires run from the faucet. The stars run away from a sky the color of bruises.

Early morning I'd wake for school and find my father, eating sal-tines and apricot jam, peach jelly or when they were in season, nectarines. I guess that's why I hold him, that time of day, in my mind like that: in orange-ish light. I'd be on my way out to school, in that first twilight of the day, early morning, the saddest time for me, and there he'd be, his chair pulled into our breakfast nook, where these days there are too many chairs with no bodies, just tragic indentations of forms: my mother's, my grandmother's, even my father's—since most days he just rolled his chair up to the table or ate his food in front of the living room t.v. And those chairs stayed empty, even mine, when I came home from school, slapped a sandwich together and took it to my room.

"Winter-girl," my father said, "hit those books hard, you're a smart one like your mama."

"I will, Daddy," I said for the millionth time, "I will," passing a dry kiss over his head.

I remember a vacation once, I was so small and Mama was wear-ing a sundress, too dressy for camping out in the desert. I remem-ber it was so windy on the first day, and the pale red color of that dust and the wind picking it up, gossamer against the air, thin red, breath of blood, striking at me and dad's chair with a little glistening sound. I remember Mama was mad at the wind be-cause of her hair and the pretty dress. I think I remember these things but I was young and I play this memory over in my mind a lot, add things and forget things, make it up as I go along with the things I'd wished in place of the things that were. I remember she sang that night, the sad song about darling Clementine, lost forever, dreadful sorry Clementine. And I was crying, not about the lost miner's daughter, Clementine, but because I was up way past my bedtime and I was confused and happy and too excited to sleep. I remember the campfire and the sticky pop sound my thumb and finger made from the toasted marshmallows I'd eaten off a pine stick earlier. The same little pop sound I could hear when my parents kissed in the dark, their one sleeping bag rustling like the flat silk ripple of wheat in a field, my daddy's sleeping legs braiding my mother's. I used to think of her all the time. Her name—how it was nighttime—but my mama was like the first sundresses of summer—not the shock of bare arms or the new thrill of flesh again, but the empty dress hung in a window with its fabric of hopeful colors, the gardens incandescent with light and the wire skeleton of a clothes hanger, framing the vacancy.

It's the beauty we miss the most, the soft smell of her perfume, the pretty sandals lined up on the floor of their closet, her beautiful hair, brushed out every night with beautiful hairbrushes, made of bronze and mother of pearl with a brass rose wound comb and a hand- held mirror with metal flowers on the back that looked like little gold fists against creamy satin, all on a mirror tray sitting on the blonde wood of her dresser. It was the sweet breath of leaving, too sweet like embalming fluid or the flowers in the mortuary, aromatic, and gaudy and heartsick that left those chairs there, year after year. My father and I worked around her things as if she were a ghost, threaded our lives around her absence, made it the centerpiece of the house and moved carefully, quietly around it so as not to tip one more thing over with no one to pick up the mess. My mother's absence was a Maypole and we held the streamers, braided our lives around it, lived in a sleepwalking daze and I swore I'd paint my own house purple some day, plant crazy gardens everywhere, color on the walls, anything but that god-awful silence.

Bone-secrets of the moon.

"I felt the truck rise a little. I felt the truck lift up a little and I was sick inside, just sick. But I couldn't do a thing, I didn't even try to help. I'm saying, I did nothing, Winter, nothing."

"Sunny," I said, "what is it?"

"It's just that we're moving," she said to me.

Sunny moved away in ninth grade, the first year of high school. It seems her father couldn't stand the house anymore with her mother's dishes and her mother' needlepoints and cross-stitches everywhere. I stood at the end of the road and watched her carry loads of things out to her daddy's truck. I watched the truck pull away from the curb and I think I saw Sunny looking hard at me, waiting for me to come closer, say goodbye. I stood there a long time, just that way, as the truck pulled off and long after, when the light leaving the sky made the house look abandoned. Then I went inside to tell my daddy my idea. I found him by the kitchen window staring out and drinking. I hadn't even finished before he smacked me just once, across the face and hard enough to leave the pink flare of an angry hand blazing for hours after. Before she left, Sunny told me her daddy wanted to move on from this place, find somewhere new where he could find a new life, maybe remarry. I thought of my father all these years alone, how strong his arms were from lifting himself in and out the chair, the bath, how quiet the house must be all day long with me in school.

"Daddy," I began, "maybe you should try to get out of the house a little bit, try to meet some people, maybe you could find a lady."

Then the sound of a ball cracking against a bat, a splash of light and my face all hot and stinging. Later in the mirror, a little seacoral shape stained one cheek.

"What do I need a wife for?" More than the slap, his voice hit me, made me sick just then, its high-pitched plea, the fury of it, the weakness behind all that.

"I have my liquid lady and she suits me just fine," he said and traced the curves of the bottle with both hands flat against the glass making a shape like a bell down then in and back out again, the way a Coca-Cola bottle was even though his whiskey bottle wasn't shaped like that, not exactly. A sleazy move that embarrassed me for him—like some random man spitting on himself outside a bar. Someone I'd speed by to avoid embarrassing us both. Someone I didn't want to know.

Behind that voice, another. "Nothing, Winter, nothing." As if I knew before I knew that anyone could pass right through us in that house with no one able to do a thing about it.

This is the way I remember: in dismembered parts, scenes from a dream, parsed-up shots like in the skin flicks Raphael and Raoul would watch in the basement, their faces gone slack and serious at once, so when I'd come down the stairs with a message from my father they'd only half-turn away from the movie with bits of body filling up the small square of their t.v., their beers tipping forward in their hands, urine-yellow and spilling to the dirty brown carpet.

Upstairs, Grandmama was humming her way down the hall, "They come to me at night, they take out my heart."

"Crazy old woman," said my father, "stop your crazy talk."

"That's the last thing I said to her," my father choked on the words as he tried to explain.

"Tipped over." Grandmama tipped over in a way that would almost seem deliberate to me later, then the raw tumble of her, the body gaining velocity in its tumble to a flight.

Nothing made sense, I could hear Sunny's voice in my head *I felt the truck give rise*, and my grandmother's body felt like it tipped end over end thirty times before she reached the foot of the stairs.

She spent three days like a wax statue, three days with that glazed look; then she was gone.

"What does it matter?" my father said after he got home and liquored up. "That woman had more bats in her belfry than the bell tower at the Cathedral of the Madeleine. That was no life."

That night I walked away from the house, far enough to make the windows the size of postage stamps, far enough so that one thumb could cancel any of the lit squares representing a room in that house. One thumb held up to the sky and block each part of the house, blot it out, rub it into the darkness around it.

With one thumb, I took them out, room by room, the kitchen cranny with all those vacancies, my bedroom window, Layla's room with lotions separating into thick curdled cream, bad buttermilk, discolored water and murky oil—then the basement where Raphael had stopped saving me, each room canceled out with one stubby thumb.

"What does it matter?" my father had said over and over—his voice staggering behind each antiseptic breath.

But I could tell he was lonelier already, as if each leaving took a piece out of him. I wanted to stay and try to tell my daddy that there are leaving women, the kind he always loves, Mama and Grandmama and me. The kind that if you try to keep them back, fly away somehow—they find a way to fly, like grandmama's mind flew from itself, a white, white bird into cold air, and mama's pretty dresses left behind, hanging from their frail shoulders, and me at the edge of town, thumbing a way out.

❧ *Invunche y Voladora* ❧

ROY KESEY

1. Llamas

As they wake in their rented cabin on the first day of their honeymoon in Chile, they realize, first the wife and then the husband, that they remember nothing of the wedding or reception. Neither mentions this to the other. The fire in the woodstove is dead, the cabin is very cold, and there are a dozen llamas gathered outside. No one told the spouses there would be llamas in Chile.

The llamas, their delicate necks, their long lashes, their great soft eyes—they stare in through the massive bay windows as the spouses shower and dress, make breakfast and eat. The spouses prepare to leave, and the llamas mass in some sort of spiraling formation. The spouses step out the door, and the llamas attack.

Does the wife scream out? Does she panic in any way? She does not. The husband screams slightly, however. The spouses take up thick sticks of firewood from the rack by the door, they wield their firewood mightily, and slowly they drive the spiraling, spitting, biting beasts away, bleeding about the face and head, the llamas and spouses, all of them bleeding. Later the cabin manager will apologize for the incident. It must have been something they ate, she will say.

2. Fishing

The spouses' guidebook says that Chile has some of the finest trout streams in the world, but the spouses do not go fishing. They do not know how to fish and are not anxious to learn. They drive over many, many streams on their way to other places, and occasionally stop to take pictures.

As they drive, the husband begins to remember. The wedding is still blurred, but the reception line afterward comes clearer: the hundreds each with glass in hand, the congratulations and thanks, the many old women in old fur coats—or was it only one old woman, one old fur coat, and she passed through the line many times?

3. History

He is American, she is Peruvian; her eyes are onyx and his are shale. Three months ago she was pregnant, and both were thrilled and terrified. In eleven furious weeks they planned everything: wedding, reception, honeymoon. Then her blood came, and not just her blood. At the hospital the bleeding was stopped and the news was given: the child was gone. And the fiancée had been damaged, somehow. Not only not now, then, but never. The wedding was six days away.

4. *Skiing*

—Take me back to the lodge.

—You can't quit now.

—Yes I can. Take me back to the lodge.

—Honey, we—

—I'm cold and I'm tired and I want to go back to the lodge.

—I'm not taking you back to the lodge.

—Yes you are.

—No I'm not.

—Fine, I'll go by myself.

—You can't.

—Yes I can.

—No you can't. You don't know how to take off your skis.

—Take me back right now.

—No.

—I hate you.

—I know. I don't care. You can't just quit.

5. *The Lake*

After only a moment or two of staring at a lake beneath an overcast sky, one begins to see the dark shapes. Each time one looks away they rise up and slap down on the surface, creating unnatural wakes.

All day long as the spouses nurse their bruises, the lake is scarified by low wind, and the dark shapes writhe. The cabin manager tells the spouses that the shapes must be large fish or cloud-shadows.

6. *Puerto Varas*

The spouses pack their bags and load them into their rental car and drive two hours farther south, to another cabin with bay windows and a woodstove. There is another, much bigger lake. And there is a volcano, or so the spouses have been told, but the volcano, the volcano out the massive windows, the volcano across the lake, it is invisible. There is not enough light to see.

The spouses wake on their first morning in the new cabin, and still the volcano is invisible, obscured now by clouds. This lake, too, is scarified by low wind, and the dark shapes rise and fall.

—Well, says the husband.

The wife nods, yawns, stretches beautifully, curls into him, goes back to sleep.

The husband stares out at the lake.

7. *Horseback*

As they wait for the guide to saddle the horses, little by little the husband remembers still more. She came in on her father's arm, and the statuary trembled; painted figures looked, and were amazed. Her father was in full dress uniform, long sword bright at his side, and the almost-husband wished that he had a sword, too. But it didn't matter. She came to him all the same.

Now they are on horseback, it is raining and he is petrified. This was his idea, was supposed to be amusing, but the horses have been rested long and well on high pasture: they want to run. The husband had no idea that this was how it is, the tremendous speed through thick trees, the branches that reach for him. Every so often the guide catches up to him, rips the reins from his hands and leans back. The horses stop simply. But when the husband tries the same trick, his horse runs still faster, the wind and rain, he is numb and slipping from the saddle as the guide saves him yet again.

They ford a river, the water fast at the withers, and then they are climbing and the horses must walk. Above them hawks circle, and the husband remembers, the *Blue Danube* over and over, and he danced with his wife, her mother, his mother, her grandmother, his sister, her aunt, another of her aunts, still another, the *Blue Danube* endlessly, spinning and spinning and spinning like these hawks.

The rain has stopped. There are striations of sun through the varying grays.

—Look, says the guide.

They turn and look. The river is silent five hundred yards below them. The far lake is a gem of ten thousand facets. But even from here the volcano cannot be seen, is still cloud-shrouded and blind.

They take a different trail back to the stable, and the horses are content to walk, fern and pine and berry. The husband reaches out, takes the wife's hand as they amble downward. The spouses smile though their bottoms are very sore.

The husband tenses, there is a new smell, acrid and musky, and then his horse bolts. He clenches his legs to the horse's sides, hauls back on the reins but the horse gathers speed into trees, over snags and deadfall, into a clearing and there is an old wooden bridge, the husband drops the reins, wraps his fists in the horse's mane and prays as they're onto the bridge and it slants to one side, the river and rocks beneath them, the far end of the bridge, one piling is loose, the bridge wavers and shakes and they jump, the horse stretches out, they make the far side and the husband tumbles heavy into ferns.

He lies there on his back. Most parts of him ache, but nothing drastically, nothing in a fractured way. He stares up through bracken. The guide arrives, and the wife, breathless.

—What the hell was that? asks the husband as he gets to his feet.

—The urine of the puma, says the guide. It makes the horses afraid.

—Oh. Well.

—That bridge is a so dangerous place. You should have crossed through the water as we did before.

—All I did was hang on.

—This is not a ride for the beginners. Why did you say me that you are expert?

The husband glares at the bracken. Then he turns to face his wife. To his surprise her eyes are bright. Perhaps she saw how he jumped, how he cleared the broken bridge, how he flew. She smiles and now he knows: she saw.

8. Salmon

The ache, the pain, the tiredness: all this can be overcome. Other things cannot, and still the spouses try. Miracles happen, they believe, or there would not be a word for them. They hope. That is their one bulwark in this world. Despite the doctor's words, they believe it is not an impossible thing. They can hope. They have that right.

Today they go to a lodge with thermal baths, and a restaurant said to be the best in southern Chile. They spend hours in the baths, massaging one another's aches. They talk of the wedding reception, and each memory feeds the next. The marvelous marbled hotel, though the hall itself was low-ceilinged and unattractively carpeted. The tables, the flowers, the guests all glorious. The band members in tuxedos on stage, the long sweep of truffles, and the cake.

The cake! They forgot to cut their cake!

They laugh, and groan at their aches, and laugh, and thank each other for the good massage. Yes, they forgot to cut the cake, but perhaps it was cut later, by others, after the husband and wife had left.

And the food, how delicious the food must have been, the food they took so long in choosing, the food so splendidly arrayed, the food neither spouse had time to taste. The five wines he picked, the Pinot Noir, oh yes, and the fine hors d'oeuvres she selected, the prosciutto and stuffed artichoke hearts, all of it gone now forever, but delicious, it must have been delicious.

The spouses withdraw from the baths, towel one another dry, dress and proceed to the restaurant. The salmon cuts are massive and select. The wine is right. The lighting is subdued, the waiters attentive, the mousse precise. Things look good for another try.

Back in the cabin the wife goes to shower and the husband builds a fire. The pyramid of twigs, the single match, the thicker twigs, still thicker, and the thinnest of split branches. He stretches, pours two glasses of wine, adds more branches and a small log. It is an outstanding fire.

The shower sounds have ended, and there are other sounds now. Guttural gurgling sounds. He knocks on the bathroom door.

—Give me a minute, says the wife.

—Are you okay?

—Not really. I think the salmon—

More guttural gurgling sounds. The husband opens the door, steps in, is hit by the smell but staggers on. He rubs her back as she rids herself of the last of the salmon. She rinses her mouth and he rubs in small circles. He takes her to bed and returns to clean, the grayish orange everywhere, the specks of garlic and oregano, he wipes it all away.

9. The Day of Rest

The husband reads his Darwin, the notebooks from the voyage to this very region, and stares out the bay windows at where the volcano must be. The dark shapes turn and roil and heave beneath the surface of the lake.

And the wife in bed remembers other things. The night of their wedding coincided with the birthdays of five of their guests, and the five men gathered at the reception and were sung to. It was improbable and fine, and the voices rang out in that low-ceilinged hall, the band joined in and the toasts were dignified and sure. Then as they left, husband and wife, arm in arm, the cake forgotten and uncut, as they made for the door the guests began to applaud, louder and louder, the applause rose and swirled around them, as if they had done a marvelous thing, and they had, oh they had.

10.Yogurt

—You always do that.
—Do what?
—You never think about anyone but yourself.
—What are you talking about?
—How many yogurts did you just put in the basket?
—Three, I think.
—And all of them for you.
—I—
—What flavor are they?
—Um. Vanilla.
—I can't believe you would do that.
—Why are you making such a—
—You know I don't like vanilla.

—Yes, okay, but couldn't you just——
—Of course I could. That's not the point.

11. Farther South

She now understands how it will be. When the act is done, when they fall flushed and smiling to their respective sides, the hope lasts only a few seconds more. Soon it will not last even as long as the act; then they will give in, and it will be gone. She turns to him, and he closes his eyes. She puts her hand on his chest, and he puts his hand over hers, and does not open his eyes.

They pack their bags again and drive still farther south, toward the island called Chiloé. On this day at last the sun comes fully out, the lake glints and no dark shapes appear. On the far shore stands the white-tipped volcano, not quite as tall or jagged as the spouses had imagined.

The roads are lined with eucalyptus, and in every field are the bandurrias, long-necked and duck-sized and many-colored; they keen and take flight as the spouses drive past. She teaches him the *Padre Nuestro*, and he teaches her the *Star-Spangled Banner*. Hours pass easily.

To Puerto Montt, and then to Pargua where the ferry waits. The spouses drive into the maw, park, climb to the upper deck and stand in the whipping wind. The clouds over Chiloé are dark but the air above the channel is clear. The island is a distant low bank of green. The ferry eases away, swarmed by seabirds.

At the dock in Chacao, the spouses drive out the far side as the rain begins, lightly now but thickening. They take a wrong turn, end up in a cul-de-sac, and there is a church. The church is closed. Beside it is a sign: Kilometer 0. So it is from here that one might begin.

On the road to Ancud the spouses keep watch for the invunche,

Guardian of the Cave, a coarse-haired monster fed on human flesh, head spun half a turn on its neck, one hand sewn into the muscled back—the spouses have done their homework, read their Chatwin. But they see no such thing, and are slightly disappointed.

Slowly the rain thins over acres of conifers and bare hardwoods. The hills are green, and the guidebook tells the spouses to be reminded of Ireland, a place they've never been. Along the highway that rises and falls are solid walls of hedge flecked with small yellow flowers, and men ripping into the walls with chainsaws. The men are red-cheeked but dark-skinned, short and strong and weathered. The spouses stop to ask.

—Espinillo, say the chainsaw men. A plague. The roots run deep and spread. Impossible to eradicate, no matter how hard you try.

It is the most beautiful plague the spouses have ever seen. They thank the men and get back in the car. Cattle in fields, old farmhouses leaning north, loose mountains of firewood. In Dalcahue they find an open café, are served by a crook-toothed waitress, and the sun breaks through.

Arriving in Castro they seek out the waterfront. They have heard of the houses here, and the houses are just as they've heard: stilted, absurdly colorful, purple and blue and orange and gold, and green, like Ireland. The spouses take all the right pictures.

The city is hilled and densely built. At the top there is a hotel, and a room, the bed is small but well-blanketed and the spouses fall deeply into it.

12. Blisters

The Spaniards held Chiloé for three hundred years after they'd lost the rest of southern Chile to the Mapuche counterattack, says the guidebook. For three hundred years the Chilotes built everything with the wood at hand. Houses, churches, ships: just wood and what could be managed, what could be dreamed up and done.

Castro is filled with small stores selling weavings, carvings, jewelry of semiprecious stones. The wife buys dozens of gorgeous useless things as the husband stares out the windows and attempts not to sigh. She pauses, lapis lazuli paperweight in hand, remembering the two families lined in the front of the church, his family and hers, overwhelmed, joy-smitten and bright. She buys something for everyone, forgets no one from either family, and the husband is astonished and humbled and bitches about the weight of the bags.

For the next three days they explore the national park. Along the Chepu past Coipomó, the spread of underwater forest, dead branches reaching from the river. The spouses hike down the coast, dune and cliff, petrel and puffin and gull. Then the southern sector, a pair of otters on the bank of the Anay, and a tiny deer: pudu, says the guidebook—the size of a spaniel. Into the vast stands of larch and myrtle, the vines and bromeliads, in as far as they dare to go, a step further, another.

They drive back to Castro and their hotel each night. Blisters have risen on the wife's feet, but she says nothing to the husband. As she watches him twitch in his dreams, she listens for a flurry of wing-beats: voladora, the Messenger, who vomits out her stomach and intestines, grows wings and flies shrieking over the villages of Chiloé each night, searching for the near-dead whose souls might soon be harvested. When night is done she returns to her lair, re-digests her insides, takes human form again and rejoins her family. But the wife hears nothing of the sort, and at last she sleeps.

The next day as they walk, her blood comes, or something like it. She steps into a dense copse to do what can be done, and the husband waits in a clearing. He hears a slight rustle; a moment later a bird appears, diminutive, red-breasted, tail cocked as it hops from cone to branch. The husband remembers what he's read: chucao, the prophet-bird, with three distinct calls. *Chiduco*, a sign of good fortune. *Huitreu*, presaging disaster. The third, which Darwin tried and failed to remember as he wrote, this is the call that the husband hears now.

13. What Awaits

Work awaits. It is time for the drive to Santiago, the flight back to Lima. The husband squints and grunts as he loads the luggage, pausing to work out the geometry of the thing, the lengths and widths and depths, so that everything will fit cleanly, so that nothing will shift on the way, and the wife remembers the sight of his face as he lifted her veil; she stares up at the clear sky and dreams of him as her invunche, the guardian of their cave, and she as his voladora, bringing him secrets, the truths that will carry them both.

When their plane lands in Lima, at the baggage carrousel there will be a woman, dark-skinned and black-eyed, thick braids and layered skirts, short and round and pleading. She will be holding a baby wrapped in embroidered cloth, and hers will not be the normal pleading, the begging for money or food, the baby held up as proof of her need. No, this woman will be pleading differently.

—Take my child, she will say.

The infant, will it be a boy or a girl? There will be no way to tell: it will be deep in its wrappings. The spouses will look at each other. The husband will explain to the woman that they cannot possibly care for her baby. He will pull out his wallet, but the woman will not accept the offered bills.

—No. Take the child. Please. Just take the child.

The husband will insist, as will the woman. The wife will remain silent, watching.

The woman will turn, will see the approaching policeman, will push the baby into the wife's arms, will go to the policeman and berate him for bothering someone as poor as herself. The spouses will look at each other again, will search one last time for their suitcases, and as the policeman sees the baby in the wife's arms and tries to step around the serrana who insults him, obstructs him, beats at him with her short strong arms, the husband and wife will thread themselves into the crowd, will run, and their luggage will appear just then, will spin on the carrousel, around and around, like the hawks, like the music of the *Blue Danube*.

❧ *Malika* ❧

GLORIA DeVIDAS KIRCHHEIMER

What a coup, to get these two on my show together. He's notoriously shy, they say. He hides behind his photographs. She on the other hand will go anywhere, speak anywhere, tell her story to any group or persons willing to listen. She's on a mission. What she has to tell has never appeared in any nationally published newspaper. And although he has been to almost every God-forsaken war-torn place in the world, he's never been to the secret places where she was incarcerated for so many years. He passed through her country shooting the riots and refugees, but never the inner sanctum of the walled town where those horrific events took place.

Posters of her circulate clandestinely in her country but here we'll use them as background on the set along with some of his photos, maybe the Romanian orphans working in the sulfur pits, or how about the beggars with arsenic poisoning, maybe a few piled up corpses in Rwanda. The powers that be don't want to upset the television audience so we'll get the graphics people to put some swirls and transparent panels in continuous motion in front of the photos. It will be easier to segue into the car commercials, not so much of a shock. A respectful audience will be seated far enough from the participants, they'll be almost invisible.

We sent him a copy of her memoir but I don't know if he's read it. When I told her I was considering inviting him, she knew immediately who he was: Alvaro Bok is one of the greatest photographers of our time, a documentarian of the world's tragedies as she generously put it. He'd never heard of her, Malika Fawaz. Well, that's to be expected.

It wasn't easy for me to get approval for this program. *Bernie Allegro's Roundtable* is one of the last live talk shows left and that's because I refuse to have it pre-taped. Who wants to see pictures of disasters, who wants to hear about torture, the producer said. And you're not going to show his pictures of starving infants, are you? The ratings are going down, we need something upbeat. Translation: Keep the corporate honchos happy. But I have had it with teenage icons and their bare navels and the way they run off at the mouth about the older generation. And how many self-indulgent, smug unshaven novelists and filmmakers can I be polite to? I gave them my ultimatum. If I can't do this show then cancel my contract. I'll retire and write a book.

A book about the network? the boss smirked. Just try it.

My reputation was at stake. But I held out and won. Should be fascinating. Must do my homework. Too bad I couldn't get them to eliminate the commercials just this once.

The third guest on Bernie Allegro's show is Ezra Konigsberg, a social scientist at New York University who's been on the program before. To sweeten the invitation, Bernie promised to plug Ezra's latest book, a popular history of oppression in the last 25 years.

Bernie met with Malika and Alvaro for fifteen minutes before the show to prep them on timing and procedures. Ezra knew the routine from previous appearances and skipped the briefing. Bernie made it clear that the conversation would be spontaneous. Anything could come up. There were no censors here. Malika smiled brightly. She knew a lot about censorship. Her brother had run afoul of the censors with his underground newspaper and died in prison. How she envied Alvaro's ability to go into anarchic, terrorist states and take photographs, unmolested. A press pass was equivalent to a laisser passer, enabling him to move from zone to zone.

For her appearance on the program, Malika Fawaz is wearing skintight leather pants, boots, a silk blouse. She's refused makeup. Her face is an open book. She won't hide it behind a veil or chador or burkha or cosmetics. Those days are over. Here they've given her asylum. If she went back to her country today she would be arrested. They have agents here, she knows. But nothing would be accomplished by having her meet with "an accident." These days they are too concerned with their image as an evolving democracy and attracting American investors. There is no one left at home of her family to punish. They took care of that a long time ago when she was in solitary confinement.

She worries that even her memoir is passé. If Americans read that rock music is now played in the cafes of her home town, her credibility will be diminished. But the US publisher was insistent that she write the book. Write it in French if necessary and we'll get it translated quickly. Memoirs are hot, her editor told her when he took her to lunch at some obscenely priced restaurant in midtown where the waiters all wore turbans. She needed the money. And wanted to tell her story even if it was to a disbelieving audience. So this appearance on the talk show was welcome in a way. The French edition had come out simultaneously.

She reminds Alvaro of the red-light district in Jakarta where he photographed the prostitutes displaying themselves in the dimly lit windows of their cubicles. Doesn't she know that this kind of clothing is wrong, unseemly, especially for a woman who has undergone the kind of humiliation she describes in her re-markable book which he read just the night before, barely finish-ing it by daylight. There is something endearing in her lack of awareness.

"You have often been accused of beautifying suffering," said Bernie after a brief introduction of his guests. "Your photos hang in muse-ums and don't appear in daily newspapers as part of reportage. Isn't there a contradiction then between your subjects—famine, war ca-sualties, refugees—and the exquisite results of your work?"

Alvaro hated this question. This was how he worked. He found the right moment, the right lighting, worked hard for the most effective composition. He strove to make his pictures beautiful. Before he could open his mouth and answer this stupid question, Malika leaned forward and spoke. She had a chipped tooth, he noticed. It marred what was still a beautiful face.

"Mr. Bok—Alvaro—conveys tragedy in the most powerful way possible— through art." She cited examples through the ages: Goya, Picasso, Kollwitz. "I have been immensely moved by Alvaro, his photos."

Ezra brought the tips of his fingers together and raised them before his face, as though beseeching the others for their indul-gence. "Might one not consider you a voyeur?" he asked the pho-tographer. "You transgress these zones of alterity and appropriate them. In the process you make us voyeurs."

"Que'est-ce qu'il dit?" Malika was bewildered. Before he could stop himself Alvaro touched her shoulder lightly and leaned across the table. He despised these academics. How, he asked Ezra, how was it a matter of "appropriating" these terrible scenes by record-ing them and making them available to the world.

"Well, let's take Malika—" said Ezra. "Ms. Fawaz," Bernie quickly interjected. "—Ms. Fawaz. She was a participant. She suffered, she was tortured, imprisoned…" Alvaro glanced at Malika to see if this clod was eliciting a reaction. She remained stony-faced. "And she didn't have the immunity that you had with your press pass."

That was true, said Alvaro. "I am humbled every time I travel through these places. I don't know if I would have the courage…" Her book had shaken him. Would he have been able to hold out during interrogation? She was looking down, twisting a silver bracelet round and round. There were scars on her wrist.

"Surely we all agree," Bernie said, "that writing this memoir was an act of bravery. Not only to have undergone these…" He was at a loss for words. "How do you characterize a torture chamber. Sadistic guards. Erosion of the personality day after day."

"I wrote it quickly," she said harshly. "There was no art in it. It was my personal history. It is only 150 pages, it passes quickly and then people go about their business. It is nothing lasting."

"We need to take a moment's break," Bernie said cheerfully while fuming that the next thing viewers would see would be a van careening around a desert road.

During the commercial, Bernie offered his guests some mineral water. No one spoke.

"When you consider the portrayal of resisting The Other…" said Ezra after the break. But it was as though Ezra wasn't sitting at the same table. He was outside. He was "the other." Malika's lashes, Alvaro noticed, were immensely long. Her hair had grown in luxuriously, remarkably, considering what had happened to her in the prison.

"You, Alvaro," she said, "your work is for posterity, it will always be there. To remind and elevate us. I am just one of many people who had the bad luck to be in a bad place." She'd seen many of his photos even before she knew that they would meet. His work was on exhibit in major museums. And now here he was, the man himself, self-effacing, lean, all in black, a man of perhaps fifty. A dimly-remembered sensation rippled through her.

"Not to detract from your work, Alvaro," said Bernie, patting his signature red tie, "but the beauty of your photos, their—one could almost say, perfection—might raise the suspicion that the images have been doctored electronically." He liked to play devil's advocate. It led to provocative discussions. "News organizations use computer tweaking almost as a matter of course."

"Did you bring me here to insult me?" Alvaro asked, clenching his fists.

Bernie backtracked quickly. He didn't mean to imply… But, he thought, he had to get something out of the idea. He smiled. "Forgive me, but if you are so much against using the tools available, you could be accused of being old-fashioned. Doesn't that disturb you?"

"No." End of subject for Alvaro.

Bernie quickly turned to Ezra—equal time for everyone was the rule here. Ezra was a specialist in a new field called the sociology of suffering. Would he be kind enough to define it for their viewers?

Ezra leaned back, enjoying himself now that he had the floor. "The etiology of suffering encompasses the effects of discrimination, of war, of natural and man-made disasters." A conference had recently taken place on "The Sociometrics of Suffering" in Villa Antinori on Lake Garda, Italy, a beautiful spot. The villa had formerly been owned by Andrew Carnegie. Participants came from all over the world; some invited guests of course could not attend because the repressive regimes under which they live would not permit them to leave. "We even had one of your people, Ms. Fawaz. Professor Abu Jelloun. He had no difficulty getting a visa."

"Why should he?" Malika said. "He's part of the government's inner circle. Before he became a professor he was attached to the secret service. He knows me."

"Many people know you now," Bernie said smoothly, "thanks to your remarkable book." He signaled for the book to be shown onscreen. After a long enough interval to enable the slow readers to take in the jacket copy, he turned the conversation to Alvaro's development as a photographer. Who were some of his major influences, he asks. He was a little startled not to hear the familiar names of Henri Cartier-Bresson or Jacob Riis or Walker Evans, but instead those of the very artists cited by Malika. "Getting back to the question of being a voyeur, Alvaro…"

"Whoever is watching this program can be described as a voyeur, don't you think?" Malika said. "Look at what we're talking about. Don't you think some people are titillated by implications of sadism and torture leavened by an occasional advertising break?"

Ungrateful woman, Bernie thought, preparing to wrap up the show. "We have time for a couple of questions from our call-in audience. Yes—?"

"Hi—I'm John from Terre Haute. That's Indiana in case you don't know. Question for Mr. Bok. Why do you photograph only scenes of tragedy? Why don't you shoot normal people?"

He'd been asked this question so often. His stock answer: my subjects were by and large "normal" until their normality was taken away from them. Not for the first time did Bernie think that it was a mistake to include call-ins. The staff that screened the calls were only interested in geographical diversity. Most questions were obvious. But that's what the producers wanted. The lowest common denominator, Bernie thought resentfully.

"Hello, I'm Xenia from Plattsburg. What's your favorite camera lens? I'm asking because I have a Leica M6 that gives me a lot of trouble. For instance—"

Bernie cut in and said almost apologetically that questions of a technical nature could be addressed to the program in writing. "Last question?"

"This is for Malika. No, I don't want to identify myself. I think she's making up half of her stories—"

Malika waved frantically at Bernie to cut off the caller. She recognized his accent. He could be one of them, the secret police.

Time was up, Bernie announced, catching on to her panic and pushing the cutoff button. Music came up. "In the following weeks, we will meet with the following guests…"

Alvaro was speaking French to Malika even though they were still on the air. He seemed to be taken with the woman who was admittedly a beauty despite her gaudy clothes. "Si on sortait après, prendre un verre…?" Alvaro murmured.

Look what's going on here, Bernie thought. He can't keep his eyes off her and vice versa. Talk about voyeurs, what's the audience thinking. Bernie held up Malika's memoir, the English edition, then a large coffee table book of Alvaro's factory photos taken all over the world. And Ezra's study, *Reconceptualizing Dissonant Optimization.*

Sometimes participants sat around after the telecast but Bernie needed to get home, have a drink, wait for the producer's call which he wasn't too sanguine about. Ezra shook hands with the other two but held Malika's hand a little longer than necessary. "Perhaps we might meet for dinner if you are remaining in town … ?" he said softly.

On the make, Alvaro thought disgustedly. Or maybe he wants to do a case study of her. Alterations of dream patterns based on having a 100-watt light on 24 hours a day, while an incessant tape plays the cries of victims.

She, docile now, demurely polite, waited until Konigsberg let go of her hand. "Perhaps," she said. "We will see." He made her take his card before they parted outside the studio near Central Park.

It was only after three months that she was able to tolerate Alvaro's hands on her bare skin. What did she see when she looked at him? The men in and out of uniform who had tormented her. He understood. She shed copious tears of apology. "I want to and yet I cannot." Each time she removed her clothes, the pain came back to her. At the same time there was a parallel agony of longing.

It was difficult for Alvaro to contemplate and not touch. If she had been plainer…but no, despite the abuse of her body she exuded a languorousness. He could examine her at leisure. A crooked toe, a small map of gashes over one shoulder blade added to the surprise of her beauty. He thought he would go mad with desire but was determined to wait until she was ready. Perhaps he could photograph her, he thought. For relief. If she would allow it.

Not the face she said. And not for publication. And not yet. He agreed. Maybe she would change her mind about publication. His agent had been after him for years to put together a collection of nudes—any kind, under any circumstances: dead, old, young, battered. It would complement his work. Add a new dimension. People would flock to see them. He could be sure of selling prints, unlike those that made up the bulk of his work.

They met in the small apartment she had sublet from a fellow dissident who was also in exile. When Alvaro was not out of the country, he stayed with her though he slept on the couch. The apartment was sunny. Street noises wafted up from the street. Sounds of normality: children calling, drunks singing, heavy trucks transporting goods from one end of the continent to the other just so that she would never want again for fresh lemons. When she was alone during those early months, she wrote letters, arranged for speaking engagements, and mostly, shopped for food and cooked, in anticipation of Alvaro's arrival.

Wherever he was, he called her. She never asked if he was "home," though he once let slip that his wife had been ill. "What are you doing?" he would ask from Dar-es-Salaam or Tblisi or Oaxaca.

She told him of her day: making curtains, walking in the park, preparing a lecture, repairing a chair.

"How domestic," he said, laughing.

"It keeps me calm," she said a little defensively. "And you—are you taking care of yourself? Are there minefields where you are?"

He would laugh. How like her to be always concerned with danger. He would have preferred her to ask first about the work he was doing. But of course the connection was poor, he would be unable to tell her everything he wanted to. They could be cut off at any moment.

Alvaro arrived unexpectedly one afternoon after an absence of almost a month, the longest he'd been away from her. Malika had given him a key because the sound of the doorbell or a knock on the door frightened her.

She whirled around from the stove when he entered. Without thinking he dropped his bags and drew her into his arms and kissed her almost brutally.

"You are crushing me," she said in a small voice.

He'd forgotten her fragility. How long was he expected to tiptoe around her? She disengaged herself and stepped back.

"I would have gone to the hairdresser if I knew you were coming," she said, her mouth trembling.

"Who cares about that?" The fixation of women on their appearance was exasperating. He'd found it to be universal though somehow he hadn't expected it of Malika.

"I am tired." Alvaro said. And he was suddenly conscious of how dirty he was. His clothes rumpled from the long flight, a two-day growth of beard. It was almost as though her concern for appearances was contagious. "Let me take a shower," he said almost belligerently.

Water. How many places had he visited where it was almost nonexistent. He'd photographed a village in Chad whose inhab-

itants had to walk for miles and then wait in line for the tank
trucks to arrive from the capital to distribute water. If I were religious, he thought, I would thank God for this water. It was almost obscene for him to have photographed children lying on
the ground with their tongues hanging out, almost dead from
thirst. Maybe there was something to what had been said on the
television discussion about being a voyeur. If that were true then
he would have to abandon his profession. Then what? Having
seen so much misery was it enough to remain an outsider, hiding
behind the camera? Earning a living from the tragedies of others? Reveling in the responses of his admirers. Now he thought
again of Malika's memoir. She had defied those in power, resisted
hideous interrogations, and almost died. He was suddenly
ashamed.

The door to the bathroom opened as he was about to turn off
the shower.

"Leave the water on," Malika said and stepped in. Alvaro swore
in French.

"Le savon—the soap." she said and turned her back. Her hair
was streaming, She raised her arms. "Do all of me."

He understood. She needed a buffer, a soothing layer of soap
between their two bodies, so there would be nothing abrasive on
her skin. Mist filled the small shower stall so that he couldn't see
her clearly. She wrapped her arms around his back. Everything
was slippery and she laughed. He hesitated. "Nothing hurts," she
whispered. "Everything is healed. You made me well."

—

"How is it," she asked him, "that you can concentrate so totally
when you work? Don't you hear the bombs, aren't you distracted
by the rain?"

"When I work, I work. Isn't that true of everyone?"

She looked at him almost pityingly. "Aren't you aware of other things going on around you? I think that if a plague of locusts descended on you, you would just brush them away and keep on taking your pictures."

He'd never encountered a plague of locusts, he said, but once a road he was on was blocked by thousands of frogs. Did that qualify? He was smiling but didn't understand her point.

"I have always admired the capacity of men to compartmentalize their lives. Everything goes in a pigeon hole. Work in cubicle number one. Sex in another. Torture in another. Family life. No crossover whatsoever."

"Are you equating me with those who victimized you?" What a peculiar path her thoughts took sometimes. Perhaps she was still having nightmares but he was afraid to ask.

His next trip was not for two weeks and therefore they were together constantly. Together they attended concerts or went to galleries and restaurants. She even dragged him shopping for pots and pans. A new corkscrew, a garlic press. A frilly lampshade.

She spent what he thought was an inordinate amount of time preparing meals for him. He asked once if she didn't find it dull, all this domesticity.

"I love it. You don't know how calming it is to have a routine, the right implements, electricity, running water. It is the relief of the ordinary. I could live like this for the rest of my life."

But not with me, he thought. He found this emphasis on mundanity stupid. It diminished her in his eyes.

One evening, at the dinner table, just before serving the soup she asked if they might say a small prayer of thanks.

"Don't be absurd. The soup will get cold."

"My darling, indulge me. I have been thinking more and more of the lack of spirituality in my life. I was brought up with religion."

Alvaro laughed. How pathetic she was sometimes. "I suppose you are going to build a little shrine with a few icons above the kitchen sink."

Tears filled her eyes. "I did not expect this of you. I was drawn to you in large part because of your compassion. It marks all your work."

"Work is one thing, and dinner is another, as you illustrated when speaking of compartments in a man's head. I think you might do well to start writing again. Didn't that Konigsberg fellow ask you for an article recently. Did you start it?"

She broke off a piece of bread and crumbled it into her soup. "He wanted something on 'reification of the identity paradigm.' These people are zombies. People are dying in the streets and all they can do is theorize."

He got up and came around to her side of the table. "Now I recognize you again." He lifted her up and they embraced while the soup got colder and colder.

Three years after Alvaro and Malika broke up she was named as the first Minister for Women's Affairs by her country's newly elected president. One of her first trips was to Villa Antinori on Lake Garda as the leader of a delegation to an international conference on women's rights. She remembered hearing about the place on the television program where she had first met Alvaro Bok. He'd had some sort of breakdown she'd heard not long ago and had stopped working.

She was not the president's first choice for the position but he had been influenced by advisors who believed that her family name would carry weight with the general population. The president had issued an amnesty to those officers who had participated in the repression. Malika had been asked not to press any charges and to support the new regime. In exchange she was promised a position in the government. She allowed herself to be convinced that she could be more useful to her country by going along with the president's policies. What good would it have done to try to bring her tormentors to trial? They would have been acquitted anyway and then they would have tried to silence her permanently. Conscience was a fragile quality, dependent on definitions. That's what Alvaro had taught her. He'd wrestled with it, as he became increasingly obsessed with the notion that he was exploiting his subjects, feeling more and more helpless in the face of the enormity of their sufferings. Her example was, he said, a reproach to him. He could never show such courage.

Malika wearied of his adulation and in a conversation that she regretted her whole life accused him of making a mockery of "conscience." Where was his "conscience" when he openly began to betray her with other women—she wasn't speaking of his wife— and never made an attempt to be discreet about it. She accused him of hurting her deliberately. She thought a man like him was above such behavior which was inconsistent with the compassion that had guided his life and work. "It isn't easy living with a holy woman," he said just before he packed his few belongings. "A holy woman who is mired in banality," he added, ripping down the kitchen curtains she had made with such devotion.

That was three years ago. Since then, she had avoided all entanglements.

For the conference at the villa, in deference to the customs of her country, she was wearing the chador even though many of the women were in Western dress. They looked self-conscious she thought, unused to revealing faces and limbs. Whereas she felt protected in the enveloping garment. It would deflect lascivious glances as it had been designed to do.

The president of her country had sent along some observers, all male, as though women still needed to be supervised, albeit benignly. Among them was the deputy vice-minister for education, now walking with a cane. She hadn't seen him in many years, not since his arrest together with her brother with whom he'd gone to school. Wally, they called him. Walid Hamad. He kissed her hand when they encountered each other in the lobby of the villa. That was certainly against protocol, she said, delighted. "Paris spoiled me," he said. "Ah—" he checked his watch "—my group is meeting to talk about training more doctors."

"All male, no doubt."

"One thing at a time," Wally said. "First get your women to learn how to read."

One of the panels was devoted to child pornography. Trafficking in children was widespread and few governments were concerned enough to control it. The "industry" as it was called had been facilitated through the circulation of photos on the Internet. Some of these were passed around to the participants. How artful they were, how innocent. They reminded her of Alvaro's photos of children except that these were posed and naked. What if, she thought, what if in his despair and decline Alvaro had turned to photographing these children. She broke into a sweat and pushed the scarf off her head. Perhaps she had driven him to it. There was an impatient tap on her arm from her neighbor who held out her hand for the pictures.

For the duration of the conference, Malika was unable to concentrate. My mind is not compartmentalized, she thought. Alvaro was occupying all available space. There was so much important work to be done here—resolutions to be passed, votes taken, mission statements, petitions. But everything was reduced in importance for her now. She began to feel feverish with longing. Where was he now? Wars were breaking out again in her region and here she was mooning over a lost lover. Headlines began to intrude on the conference. Dispatches from the capital city were ominous and it looked as though the new president might be overthrown by the military. Here was a picture of him, distinguished but haggard, in a cave somewhere, surrounded by his cabinet. Almost all the male advisors at the conference were packing up to go home. But perhaps she would be unable to return. Some journalists had been ambushed and killed.

On the last day of the conference, she saw professor Abu Jelloun who had arrived late. He sought her out. "Am I forgiven?" he asked with his charming smile. "I know you hold me responsible for what happened to your brother but believe me, I myself was in hiding at the time. I have just come from our capital. Things are not going well. Have you seen the latest?" He handed her a copy of the previous day's *Independent* from London with a story about the battle raging in their city. The front page contained a spread of battle photos. Men being blown into the air. Corpses. Wailing mothers. The photo credit read Alvaro Bok. She gasped.

Jelloun mistook her agitation. "Only pictures can convey what is happening," he said somberly. "These are a bit much." He led her to a couch and brought her some cold water.

So Alvaro had become a photojournalist, deliberately plunging into danger. Was he trying to commit suicide or had he changed his approach to his work?

The conference had been thrown into disarray. Malika's delegation was unsure whether to return home or remain in a place of safety. They looked to her for an answer but all she could think of was seeing Alvaro. It would be impossible to find him. He'd been in her country a few days earlier but who knew if he was still there. Perhaps Jelloun could help her.

"Ah yes," he said. "You were on a radio—excuse me, a television program a few years ago with Bok and that asinine sociologist. I happened to catch it and heard you make a most unflattering reference to me." He laughed. "A little publicity doesn't hurt, especially in political circles."

"Perhaps I misspoke in the heat of the moment," she said, swallowing her anger. They were strolling on the promenade along the lake. It was twilight and the jasmine blossoms were in full bloom.

Wally Hamad was walking toward them. He was about to hail her when he saw Jelloun. Abruptly he turned away and hobbled into a cafe.

Jelloun had not seen him. "So you want to locate Bok."

Her face was burning. Mercifully he didn't ask her to explain.

"It should not be difficult. I still have my contacts. I could even have him brought here. Would you like that?"

"I thought you don't engage in kidnappings any more." He was still a dangerous person despite his disclaimers.

"We'll let that pass." He looked at her with open sexual interest. "Suppose I guarantee his safety. What then?"

"I will be forever grateful," she murmured shading part of her face with the head scarf.

Bernie Allegro likes to do follow-up programs wherever possible. Much of the time it can't be done. His panelists travel or they're heavily committed or don't want a rehash of their original appearances. Luckily for him, Malika Fawaz is back in the States, in exile again though she hoped it would be temporary. Ezra Konigsberg—good old Ezra—is delighted at the invitation. His last two books are not doing well and he needs the exposure. As for Alvaro Bok, it wasn't easy tracking him down. For once, the producer was enthusiastic about the program Bernie's planned. There's a lot more history to be told about that gal and Bok has just about changed careers. Unlike the first program, this one will be taped in advance so that any awkward moments can be cut.

"Is it true," Bernie asks Alvaro after the introductions, "that you have retreated from the more tragic subjects you were known for in your photographs?"

Alvaro's cheeks are sunken, his shoulders are hunched. Where

is the tensile strength of the man she knew? Malika cannot believe that they were once lovers. He speaks haltingly now—his
eyes don't meet anybody's. He scarcely looked at her when they
shook hands earlier in the reception area. His work now, he says,
revolves around the nude, the wounded nude so to speak. Some
pictures flash on the screen: women's bodies for the most part,
scarred, lame, deformed. There's one photo—she could almost
say it was of her, without the face—she has a dent there in her
clavicle, a result of the first beating she ever received…but no, he
would not have the nerve. Or would he? "Like many uneducated
people," Malika says, smiling, "my grandmother believed that al-
lowing yourself to be photographed was a theft of your soul." She
only thought of this now, never before, not when she was living
with him. But then he hadn't photographed her—as far as she
knew.

Bernie and Alvaro talk about the turns of his career, his stint
as a battle photographer, his narrow escapes in the field. The co-
incidences that saved his life, particularly a helicopter airlift from
a cliff in Accra.

"Someone was watching over you," Bernie says clasping his
hands and looking intently at his guest.

Malika smiles. That helicopter did not come cheap. She had
met Jelloun's price, payment in advance in a room with a balcony
overlooking the sparkling water of Lake Garda. It was not as
difficult as she anticipated. During the whole time she thought
about the discussions her delegation had had to suspend and
worked out some legislation in her head while Jelloun groaned
his enjoyment of her battered body.

Konigsberg is blathering about valorizing diasporic communities and asks what she thinks. She turns to Alvaro. "I think Mr.
Bok has made the most impressive record of such communities—
the dispossessed, the homeless—anyone has ever seen."

Alvaro looks up at her and squints as though he barely recognizes her. Or maybe he's dazzled by how much more beautiful she's become, despite the graying of her hair. His secret victory is to have included the picture of her, taken surreptitiously while she was asleep, so many years ago. He will never dare approach her again. She's risen above the mundanity that brought their relationship to an end and become a person with real political power. Whereas he—he is one step away from being a pornographer. His wife is finally divorcing him. He longs for a home.

The talk is desultory. Bernie is not happy and looks forward to the end of the show. Even the questions from the call-in audience are lackluster: "Are women allowed to work alongside men now in your country?" "Do you prefer color film or black and white?"

At the end of the program, the panelists shake hands once again. "I wish you all the best, Alvaro—Mr. Bok," Malika says. Now her heart is broken again but this time with pity. He nods and leaves quickly. She drapes a silk scarf over her head and walks out, closely followed by Ezra who has begun talking to her about a book he'd like her to review for his journal. Outside in the reception area Wally Hamad is waiting.

"I'll let you know," Malika says to Ezra. "I've got a lot on my plate as you people like to say." Turning to Wally she says, "I'm hungry," and lets him take her arm for support. He finds it easier to manage his cane if there's someone on the other side to lean on.

❧ *My Polish Widower* ❧

KAREN KOVACIK

The cliché about your life passing before your eyes at the moment of death, I discovered, is only partially true. I had just sped across four lanes of traffic on Warsaw's notorious Wislostrada, when a beer truck cut me off. One minute I was braking hard behind a four-foot bottle of Okocim Porter, rumored to be the Pope's favorite brew, and the next I was sailing through the windshield of my husband's tiny Daewoo. I had time for only a few scenes from my life—an autobiographical greatest hits—before I found myself in the proverbial tunnel of light. Oddly, one of those scenes was Driver's Ed in Hammond, Indiana, taught by Mr. Krebs, the eternally patient woodshop teacher, as if death by car crash had rendered null and void my hard-earned C in the subject decades before. Had I been driving that '75 Monte Carlo instead of Tomek's fiberglass breadbox, I might well have survived. Instead, I began acquainting myself with the rights and privileges of the newly deceased. I could now spy on my husband any time I wanted.

My first glimpse of heaven's gate reminded me of Warsaw itself, specifically the Central Train Station, with its fluorescent lighting, platforms of waiting passengers, and staticky loudspeakers announcing arrivals and departures. The officiating angel, who resembled an auto mechanic in his glowing striped jumpsuit, explained that while the omnipresence would kick in immediately, omniscience would be granted more gradually. "Trust me," he said. "Sometimes it's better not to know."

I always hoped that if I preceded Tomek in death, I'd be admitted into the labyrinth of his mind. You can perceive a lot about a spouse—his appetite for jellied carp or fondness for solitary reading or devotion to friends—and still be awed by the extent to which he remains unknown. Add to the mix our linguistic and cultural differences and the fact that Tomek had spent considerable time alone before he met me. Solitude made him a watcher, not a talker. Had it not been for my garrulous, semi-coherent Polish, which propelled him to fits of extroversion, we would never have fallen in love.

The fact is that husbands and wives never love each other equally. And in my marriage to Tomek, I was the one who loved more. I with my lisping American accent, big soft ass, and dyed blonde hair that frizzed in the rain. Ever since I made him smile during our first English lesson some thirteen years ago, he had been my elegant boulevard, and I his tornado.

For that first meeting, we had agreed on Warsaw's Constitution Square, a post-Communist hybrid of massive limestone steelworkers and the neon logos of a global marketplace. The Café Hortex located there was itself a throwback to the former centralized economy, each miniature bistro table topped by a cheap porcelain sugar bowl and a drinking glass filled with a cone of worthless tissue napkins. While waiting for Tomek to arrive, I stared at my wedge of strawberry gelatin cake, attempting with all my power to resist it. Impatient waitresses swished past in their apple-green uniforms, and some grandpa at the next table hummed along with the radio. I had ample time to review the grammar and vocabulary lesson I'd prepared.

I was dressed in the wool skirt and high-necked cotton blouse that I always wore for first lessons because they minimized my ridiculous curves. My tall black boots remained home in the closet, and on my feet were flats so sensible I felt embarrassed to wear them in public.

On the phone Tomek had told me he was an architect, 33 years old, and gave his height in meters, which led me to expect a fairly tall man. In person, however, he was no more than five feet, in a blue raincoat and corduroys, with one of those small Polish shoulder bags, a kind of purse for men. I must have outweighed him by twenty pounds. That day's lesson was to be on verbs of motion—a refresher since Tomek had already studied English for five years. I poured him some jasmine tea from my pot, slopping a little onto his purse in the process, and started talking about coming and going. Maybe it was the radio's Chopin sonata unspooling its vehement silk or Tomek's blue eyed amusement at my careful lesson, but I suddenly knew we would be good in bed together. "To come has another meaning in English," I found myself explaining, then offered examples: "She was never able to come with him" and "He made me come five times in one night." That's when Tomek smiled.

Tomek was in the tea aisle at the Hala Kopinska when the call came from the city police. He'd just bypassed all the fruity herbals, the wild strawberry and blueberry I loved, in favor of the dense black grains that inspired him to flights of architectural fancy. I watched Tomek flip open the tiny *mobilnik* and answer with his typical subdued "Tak, slucham." Literally: "Yes, I'm listening." He stiffened when the policeman identified himself, a predictable reaction among Poles of Tomek's age. Then a look of

wonder crossed his face, the same perplexed curiosity he exhib-
ited when I mixed up two unrelated but similar-sounding Polish
nouns. "Yes, Carla's American. 44 years old." He didn't cry or
make a scene, but looked so pale and shaky that security didn't
stop him when he walked off with a tin of premier Darjeeling.

The sight of my petite Tomek straining against the November
wind made me wish I had proceeded with greater caution into
those four lanes of Wislostrada traffic. I longed to wrap his muf-
fler around his neck—one of those motherly gestures he despised.

It was only in the elevator to our ninth-floor flat—the narrow,
mirror-adorned lift where we hauled up groceries and argued about
French cinema and once almost made love—that my Polish husband, now my widower, permitted himself a couple of tears. I had
seen him cry on two occasions in our marriage: the death of his
favorite aunt and the time I drank one Wyborowa too many on
New Year's Eve and French-kissed a lecherous poet in the buffet
line. Of course, Tomek was not one to sniffle at a party. He drove
us home in silence, forcing me to endure the avalanche of his
disapproval and hurt, and averted his eyes during the interminable elevator ride. It was only in the bedroom, after I stripped
off my low-backed jade dress and attempted to convert everything I couldn't say into a no-holds-barred seduction that I was
stunned to see him cry. A reddening of the nose, a quick
shamestruck covering of the eyes. We were in bed, he seated with
his back to the wall, and when I noticed his tears, I pulled him on
top of me in a fierce American hug. I called him by name, I called
him beloved, I stroked his hair and neck and back and butt and
hissed in his ear, "I want to make love to show you how sorry I
am." He arched up on his elbows as if taking my measure. In his
coldest, most official-sounding Polish, he said, "You're not capable of that."

"Let me show you." I knew that mind games always aroused

him. His blue-gray eyes were already dry and alert.

"*Nie.*" The monosyllable of refusal resounded with arctic final-
ity, though his penis seemed of a different persuasion. In the end,
Tomek let me know the terms my apology would have to take: he
would thrust me very slowly sixty times. With each stroke, I was
to tell him I was sorry for kissing that horny idiot, Waldemar. I
was not to have an orgasm until or after this sixtieth stroke despite the fact that he knew very well—we had been married three
years—how to bring me to the brink. The legalistic precision of
his terms amused me, nudged me from abject to ironic. Mercy
fresh from the freezer was better than no mercy at all.

"*Jak chcesz*," I said. "As you wish."

And so it began, so we began, the first ten superficial as a blue-
print, my faint I'm sorrys rote with defiance. Around twenty, I
started to feel the architectonics of him, the subtle buttressing of
his pride, his fear of losing me. At 35, I began to cry myself, so I
could scarcely whisper the thick phrase of apology: *przepraszam.*
38, 39, random images of my love for him: the care he took when
defrosting our tiny fridge, tilting it back on an orthographic dic-
tionary, or our evening walks through the Park of Happiness, the
willows and poplars cascading toward the ground. 45, 46, his
nuanced finger on my clitoris; 50, 52, the choirloft shrieking with
sopranos; 53, his blue eyes dark with lust; 57, the counterpoint of
our breathing; 58, fighting the aria inside me, and finally, 60, 60,
60.

In the tiny, mustard-tiled kitchen, Tomek plugged in the electric
kettle, pried open the tea tin with a spoon, and covered the bottom of a glass with dense black leaves. The kitchen looked much
as I had left it. The same windowpane dishtowel hung on its
hook, and a heel of rye rested on the table, cut side down. How
odd to spy on one's own life, one's own husband. I felt like a

member of the secret police, a *tajnik,* watching him this way, for my Polish husband valued privacy above everything.

Tomek called one of his friends, an artist with a century-old apartment in the Mokotów district, to cancel their afternoon meeting. They were supposed to have been planning the new *kolorystyka* of the flat—a bolder look with ultramarine cushions and citron-colored walls. I didn't need even limited omniscience to predict that the artist, Grzegorz P., would invite Tomek over for a drink, would even pick him up since my widower, thanks to me, no longer had a car. Nor was I surprised when Tomek, surrounded by my headbands, hats, and scarves, confronted by my breakfast dishes in the drainer, accepted the invitation with gratitude.

My husband had always liked working with artists because they had feasible intuitions, and typically they bartered a painting for a design. He dreaded the dithery clients who had no sense they were ruining a teak Saarinen coffee table by cluttering it with a souvenir ashtray, week-old newspapers, and TV remote. I approached that category myself with my fondness for kiosk kitsch such as the little felt rooster that I used to display on the moderne étagère until Tomek could bear it no longer and threw it in our building's incinerator.

It happened that Grzegorz grew up in the southern mountain resort town of Zakopane, the only place in Poland where cognac was the primary drink instead of vodka or beer. So in Grzegorz's high-ceilinged flat, adorned with elaborate sconces shaped like lilies, the brandy snifters appeared immediately, along with a bottle of some high-octane Armagnac. Had I not been dead, I would have enjoyed handling one of those glassy bells, twirling the rich brown liquor within, and taking its plummy woodsmoke into my mouth. Which is what my widower was doing, seated in the straight-backed chair that his host had provided for him so he wouldn't disappear into the sofa. Grzegorz, too, was cradling a swollen snifter, his long legs in blue jeans stretched beneath the table, the beginnings of a belly spilling over his belt.

In their circle of friends Grzegorz threw the best parties and had the most women. And while he typically favored Art Academy brunettes—if the young things hanging on him at gallery openings were any indication—I more than once caught him staring at my ass. He had a surveyor's gaze, an instinct for declivity and rise. Regardless of how intelligently I managed to talk about twentieth-century painting, including his own geometrized portraits, I was always aware of that narrowing of the eyes, that sense of appraisal.

With Tomek, Grzegorz displayed none of that judicious weighing. It pleased me to watch how skillfully he maneuvered the conversation to put my widower at ease, starting out with recent Warsaw buildings. And Tomek, though he never swore in my presence because of some old-fashioned notion of courtliness, used even the most notorious Polish words for describing Roman Z.'s green monstrosity of a supermarket. Eventually, however, Grzegorz brought up the subject of my abrupt demise.

"*Co zrobisz teraz bez Carli?*" No American would ever ask a bereaved friend straight out how he'd manage now that his wife was gone, but the question seemed unremarkable to Tomek.

"God knows." Tomek swirled the brandy around in his glass. "Even though a dozen times she almost drove me to divorce."

Were I not dead, I would have grabbed that beautiful glass from his hand and flung the drink in his lap. Sure we fought, operatically even, Tomek locking himself in his room, and I swearing at him through the door in English. He was the sort of person who would measure an entire wall before hanging a single picture on it, while I would use every dish in the kitchen when preparing a three-course meal. The Polish equivalents of "Quiet down" and "Get a grip on yourself" were Tomek's favorite and absolutely enraging rejoinders to me.

"While I myself don't believe in marriage," Grzegorz said, "I must say you and she seemed content enough."

I recognized that appraising gleam. Grzegorz wanted to find out something about me, something he never dared ask while I was alive, I could feel it.

"It's just that Carla was, in many ways, a child," Tomek said. "You know what Americans are like. They're served the wrong dish at a restaurant, and it's cause for war." He sipped his drink for dramatic emphasis. "On the other hand, they can't wait to see what the Christmas Angel will bring." Grzegorz laughed at this ridiculous national stereotype which I allegedly fit. For the record, I have to say that during our entire marriage, I threw precisely one tantrum at the Restauracja Staropolska, when the waiter not only brought me a dried out schnitzel instead of the Kotlet de Volaille, but also dribbled gravy on my purple wool suit. And as for the Christmas Angel, the Polish counterpart of Santa Claus, I admit I did look forward to my annual gift, but that's only because Tomek chose so well. A red silk peignoir one year, a book of idioms the next.

Grzegorz assumed that insinuating posture once again. "But certainly, Carla *jako kobieta* loved you very much." The phrase "as a woman" dripped with innuendo.

Tomek, slouching in his chair, looked bereft. I had always wondered if the dead found comfort in the grief of the living. The answer in my case was clearly yes. Without looking up, my widower muttered, "I never knew a woman who liked it so much."

Grzegorz seized his chance. "I suppose she wanted it all the time."

Tomek nodded. "In the car, or at the movies. Even at the Filharmonia once during intermission." My widower always sweated when drunk, and he was sweating now, poor thing, a hand clamped over his eyes. His voice didn't rise above a mumble. "She was wearing that ginger perfume I loved," he said, "and some huge vulgar pearls, obviously fake. We'd gone to hear Schubert and Schumann, and by the break, Carla was so pent up she couldn't sit still." Truth is, I moaned so extravagantly in Tomek's ear that he draped his coat over our laps and slid an expert hand up my velvet skirt. It was like whole notes followed by thirty-second notes. More scherzo than lieder.

"We pretend to miss the soul or the mind," Grzegorz said, softer now. "When it's the body we can't live without."

My widower stared into his empty glass as if to confirm the truth of this remark. I thought how every night I enfolded his slender back into me, blanketing him with my scent and softness and warmth. We'd fall asleep with my nose in his hair, my hands tight around his waist. His tongue often tasted like tea. The prospect of never sleeping with him again seemed unbearable. Was this how haunting began?

While playing with one of the sconces in Grzegorz's flat, I managed to ring the bell at the reception desk in heaven. Behind the desk a window opened onto a frenetic scene. The newly arrived, pale and travel-worn, carried twine-bound parcels and dented valises up interminable escalators. But a cool pitcher of lilies rested on the desk itself, as did an enormous box of chocolates. That grease monkey of an angel in his glowing, striped jumpsuit was chewing on a cloud-colored pen. "Yeah?" he said.

"Sorry," I told him, "but I'm not cut out for this place."

"Says who?"

"Me," I said. "I miss living too much. Heretical as this might sound, I'd give it all up, even the eternal bliss, for one more night of bed with Tomek."

"Hold on, you're getting ahead of yourself." The angel looked at his fat silver donut of a watch, marked with an infinity of years instead of hours. "You'll be having relations again with your husband in 31.5 years."

Without asking for permission, I helped myself to a truffle filled with persimmon and spice. "You've got to be kidding. I want him now."

"Tough. Your old man's not due to give up the ghost till he's 75."

"How will he die?" I figured I might as well use the angel's ESP to my advantage.

"Cancer of the liver. Awful way to go, but his wife will be by his side the whole time."

"His *what?*"

"Lady, you heard me. Can't expect the guy to live like a priest for thirty years."

I didn't feel like being schooled in sexual mores by an angel. Jealousy hit me worse than a thousand windshields. I grabbed another chocolate, this one flavored with violets and champagne. How *could* Tomek marry again?

"So who's the lucky bride?" I sneered.

"Girl named Beata S., twenty years his junior. They'll meet next year at the opening of her sculpture show." He gazed again into the crystal ball of his wristwatch. "And they'll marry three months later."

I pictured one of Grzegorz's Art Academy brunettes wearing only a bridal veil, straddling Tomek on our narrow bed. To comfort myself, I imagined that she had flunked out of French and had only minimal English, though of course she'd prattle on in Polish with a native's flair.

"Will they be happy together?"

The angel shrugged. "What marriage is completely happy? Tomek will be lonely without you. He'll be impressed with Beata's sculptures, which in my opinion are a little weird, though the

Holy Spirit likes them—they're these huge black and purple gourds wrapped in fabric. She'll chat with him, make him feel appreciated, and to be honest, she's not unattractive." The angel paused to see how I'd absorbed his prophecy. I rolled my eyes.

"But soon enough," he continued, "she'll consider him an old man. Someone to be coddled and sheltered from the truth. She'll take other lovers, and Tomek will again miss you and your passion."

Hearing about my widower in this way, I felt like an audience member in some upper balcony at an opera. The story reached me from such a distance it inspired only pity and not a lightning of the soul. Now Tomek would be the one to love more.

I glared at the angel. "So I'm supposed to park myself on a cloud till he gets ready to die?"

"Truth is," he said, "you're slated for purgatory." I wasn't eligible for heaven, the angel informed me, because in life I had neglected to cultivate patience. In purgatory, I'd be obliged to wait and then wait some more. They'd assign me a narrow cell with five ticking clocks all set for eternity. I would pray rosaries, endless white beads slipping through my fingers, and meditate till my mind stilled. Regular field trips to earth would be mandatory. I'd have to watch as Tomek brewed countless pots of tea, walked alone in the Park of Happiness, and made love with Beata S.

"You'll learn," said the angel, "that you can get through desire without giving in to it." He looked me straight in the eye to drive home his point, though his voice was kind.

I reached once more into the box of chocolates. My hand closed over what looked like a petit-four adorned with a buttercup. But this time I glanced at the angel for permission. When he nodded assent, I popped the confection in my mouth and let it dissolve slowly. It was a chocolate of final things, more bitter than espresso, dashed with the salt of regret, and dense as the densest loam of the earth.

❧ *Jazz* ☙

DYLAN LANDIS

It is not true that if a girl squeezes her legs together she cannot be raped.

Not that Rainey is being raped. She doubts it, though she is not sure. Either way, it is true that the thirty-nine-year-old male knee, blind and hardheaded, has it all over the thirteen-year-old female thigh, however toned that thigh by God and dodgeball. You may as well shove Bethesda Fountain into the lake as try to dislodge the male knee.

That's where she is: on her back, on the grass near Bethesda Fountain in Central Park. Angels darken in the dusk on the fountain's dry tiers, and Rainey watches through the slats of a bench. She had started to walk the lip of the muted fountain but Richard wanted to inspect the thin silty edge of the lake.

Not far, he said. A constitutional.

How far is far, that's what Rainey wanted to know. She didn't care what a constitutional was.

The lake edge quivered and Rainey saw that the water was breathing. Richard dipped his hand in Rainey's hair and said, "You could turn the fountain on."

Richard plays French horn, and Rainey's dad says all horn play-

ers are a little strange. Rainey likes to court this strangeness because Richard is three-quarters safe, he is appreciative in ways
that do not register on the social meter, he responds invisibly,
immeasurably. She has tasted the scotch in Richard's glass. Her
dad's attention was elsewhere. Her dad was riffing on the piano
in their living room, spine straight and hands prancing, head shaking *no no no it's too good*, the man up to his shoulders in sound.
Her first taste had burned and she looked at Richard *why don't
you just drink bleach* and he smiled *try growing up first*, and she
was good at this kind of talking, eye dialogue, with nuances from
the angle of the head. Then she swallowed without wincing and
looked at Richard for affirmation and he raised his eyebrows *are
you sure you want to go farther* and she arched her neck so his gaze
would have something to slide down *I want to go far*, and she
drank the entire rest of his glass.

At the lake near Bethesda Fountain, Richard extended two
fingers with broad white moons under the nails. He tilted her
chin so she stared at his big face against the bruised sky. "You
generate energy," he said. "You could turn on a city of fountains."

The eighth-grade boys do not have pores.

Richard said, "You radiate power and light," and he led her,
electric, to the grass.

Rainey has tea-rose oil between her toes, because one day a
man might smell it there and be driven genuinely out of his mind,
and she has a wedding band on her left forefinger because her
ring finger is too small. Both of these things, the rose oil and the
ring, she claimed from the medicine cabinet after her mother got
into the cab. She looked for the plastic compact with its squashy
white dome, but that was gone.

And it is true, and only partly because of the oil and the loaded
ring, that Rainey radiates power and light. And it is true that she
loves making Richard say these things. She loves that he is a

grownup and yet he seems to have no choice. This fascinates her, just as it fascinates her that mothers look at her strangely. They are like mirrors, these mothers, the way they register the heat disturbances that emanate from under her skin.

It could be true, but it could also be a lie, that a teenage boy can get an erection just by brushing against a woman's arm on the bus. Mr. Martin in sex ed was very specific about the circumstances: boy, woman, arm, bus. As Rainey interprets this it is the Broadway bus, an old green 104 lumbering uptown at rush hour, and the woman is eighteen, no, she is twenty-one, and carrying a white shopping bag with violets on it, and wearing a lavender cardigan. The top three buttons are open, no, the top four, but it is her slender sweatered arm as she squeezes toward the back of the bus that engenders the event.

It is a lie that if a girl doesn't do something about the erection, it will hurt so badly that some injury will be caused. Mr. Martin said this too.

Rainey ran the tip of her tongue along the rim of Richard's glass and said, "When I'm sixteen, will you date me?"

"Only with your father's permission," Richard said. She waited for him to glance toward the piano, but he didn't.

It is a lie that Rainey will be allowed to live with her mother in Phoenix when she is sixteen, because her mother belongs to an ashram now, and Rainey understands that by belongs to, her mother means belongs to, the way lipstick or leotards belong to a person. It is also a lie that her father and Janet are just friends. Rainey has plastered herself to the wall outside Howard's bedroom and listened to the strange symphony of sex—the oboe of a groan, the violin singing Oh my God, the cello that is her father murmuring into some part of the body that is bent or curved.

"I take it back," Richard said. "When you're sixteen I'll marry you."

Rainey is under Richard on the grass now and she gasps from his weight, and it is true that it sounds like desire, and it is true that she likes hearing herself make the sound.

It is not true that there are boulders mashing her wrists. The boulders are Richard's hands. His hands have hair on the back. Andy Sakellarios, who might or might not be her boyfriend, has smooth hands. The boulders, like the knee, are forces she accepts for the moment. She accepts them because they are fires she has lit, and men are flammable, and Rainey believes it is her born talent, the one she sees reflected in the mothers' eyes, to set the kind of flickering orange fire that licks along the ground. Rainey accepts the pressure of the knee and the boulders like she might accept and intercept the force of a river before she lies down on its current. In Phoenix the river had been colder than cracked ice on her back teeth. Rainey let the water swirl her hair, let the cold polish her bones. She loved how surrender felt like a flower opening and she loved having the power to choose it. She ended up nearly a quarter-mile downstream where her mother found her at a campsite with boys, bikini dripping, drinking Miller from a can.

It was a lie that she had just taken one sip.

The soft grunts that squeeze from inside her are hers, but not hers. They are a lie and they are not a lie. Her toes smell delirious but Richard is crushing her lungs. Her lungs look like the fetal pigs in jars in the science room, and maybe gray like them too, because she loves to smoke. Smoking is one of the best things that ever happened to her.

"Give me that," her mother had said, and snapped the Miller can away from her, and drank deep.

The man with his knee between her legs and the heels of his palms bearing into her wrists says, "Jesus God, Rainey." He says, "I want to eat your hair."

It is a lie that he actually eats her hair, but it is true that he chews on it for a while. Her hair sounds crunchy between his teeth, like sand. She does not mind him chewing on it. She thinks how this is one more interesting thing a man can be reduced to. She wonders if sex is like math, like if you make a man want to eat your hair or go too far, does it follow that you balance the equation by letting him. And she exhales a sharp sigh whenever Richard moves, and it sounds like yes, when what she really means is let's go hear John Coltrane.

Rainey is on her back on the grass near Bethesda Fountain. There could be dogshit in the grass next to her, and Rainey wants Richard to roll off her so she can wrestle herself up, but then he might end up lying in dogshit, and this seems like terrible damage to inflict, especially on her father's best friend, who is supposed to be taking her to hear John Coltrane because her father had to play in the Village and couldn't go. John Coltrane plays three kinds of sax and he even plays jazz flute. She loves jazz flute, the way it rises hotly through the leaves of trees, then curls and rubs along the roots. Jazz flute lives about two stories off the ground. It is a reedy ache in a place she cannot name. How will Richard get her to Summerstage if there is dogshit on his back?

"Jesus," says Richard. "Somebody make me stop."

He releases one wrist and pushes her peasant blouse, with the scarlet and blue embroidery, up under her armpits. Rainey pounds on his back but her freed fist is soft as clay.

At school, where they are doing *Oedipus Rex*, Rainey has to hang herself from the climbing rope in the gym. She clutches the rope to her neck with both hands, and when she dies, Oedipus unfastens a pin from her toga. This always takes a few seconds too long because Oedipus, who is shorter than her and chubby, trembles in the face of her power and light and her breasts being so incredibly present, like an electrified fence he has to fix without touching. And then he pokes his eyes out with the pin. It is just like that Doors song where the killer puts his boots on and then he pays a visit to his mother's room, and then Jim Morrison's throat releases this unholy cry.

Through the ground, Rainey feels the crowd gathering, she feels blankets unfolding on grass, she feels tuna-fish sandwiches nestling in wrinkled tin foil. She feels John Coltrane place his fingers on the soprano sax like it is her own spine. She feels how a concert swells before it starts and she wants to be there, she wants to lie on a blanket while Richard smells her toes and is driven insane, and she wants to feel the exact moment when the sound of the sax shimmies over the Transverse and toward the sky, changing the course of the East River and starting every fountain in the city.

In Phoenix, her mother had yanked the cold-sweating Miller can away, splashing beer on the red dirt that powdered her wet feet, and said: "This is what I flew you here for? This is what your life is about?"

It is probably true that all men want to go all the way, all the time.

It is true that when Rainey has her French notebook open she is designing bikinis and maxi-coats and bridal gowns, including bridal miniskirts with trains and go-go boots, using agonizingly neat strokes with a pale pink Magic Marker. She makes the bridal gowns pink because there is no white. Is this what her life is about? It is true that she plays classical flute, and it is true that she lies and says it is jazz. She is good at drawing clothes and being Jocasta. She is good at having a disturbing and emanating body.

Richard is eating her ear now. He does it like kissing. She turns her head away but that presents the ear more centrally. She wonders when he will want to get up.

She tries to talk but all she gets out is the word "what." She wants to say, "What time is it," so Richard will leap up, wiping grass off his knees, and say, "Oh, shit, let's go." But darkness has spilled into Central Park and if she talks too loud, gangs of boys might rustle toward them carrying moonlight on their knives.

In Phoenix the boys at the campsite had been older. She told them she was fifteen and a half, that she played jazz flute and was dying for a smoke.

The boys smirked at the ground when her mother showed up. "Howard warned me to keep an eye on you," her mother said, and took a long, angry drink from the Miller can. Then she looked across the ring of stones where the fire belonged and said, "Thank you, gentlemen, for giving my daughter a beer. Did she happen to mention she's only twelve?"

"Not for long," said Rainey.

One of the boys had opened his mouth into the shape of a shocked twelve, and the blond boy with the gold earring and the cross had looked straight at her mother and said: Sorry, we didn't know. The cross made Rainey want to find the badness in this boy. She wanted to ignite him with a brush of her arm. She wanted to steal this boy from God.

"You didn't know," said her mother. She finished the Miller and crumpled the can and tossed it into the ring of stones. Rainey's mother had that ripe thing going on. Her legs were tennis-hard from another life. The boy's eyes had flickered, or maybe it was his mouth, and Rainey looked over in time to see her mother smile back, sardonic and acknowledging and quick.

Richard is licking her armpit, which she shaved on Monday with Janet's razor. Today is Thursday. She has stubble but her toes smell like tea rose. Richard raises himself so she can breathe and licks along the underwire of her Warner's Miss Debutante bra.

"Richard," says Rainey, "get OFF."

Richard says, "I'm not doing anything. I swear I won't do any-thing."

"You ARE doing something," says Rainey. He releases her wrists and she pushes on his shoulders. She wants to set fires and she wants to control how they burn. She likes going pretty far with Andy Sak, who is rendered both desperate and respectful by her power and light.

"I want to go to the concert," says Rainey. "Would you get OFF?"

She has known Richard since she was a toddler. She doesn't have to be polite.

"Five minutes," says Richard. He has freed a breast with his teeth. Rainey, propped on her elbows, sees how her breast lights up in the dark. It pumps out its resplendence like the sun. When Richard sucks on the nipple, the water roils up through the pipes in Bethesda Fountain and rains on the heads of the angels.

Rainey punches him on the head.

"Five minutes," he says. "In five minutes you'll be thirty-nine and I'll be fourteen and then we can go."

Rainey says, "Goddammit, Richard," and she is half-crying. She is not getting raped but he won't get up. She still wants to go too far but she is not sure how far is far.

"You think I just want that one thing," says Richard. "You think there's only one part of you that's special." He kisses her mouth again, and she lets him, even though he has a beard and his mouth does not have that boy-sweetness; it tastes of tobacco and steak.

Richard runs his tongue over her bare stomach.

"Thirteen," Rainey says, but there is clay in her mouth.

"I want to inhale you," Richard says. "I want to absorb you through my skin."

The current had been so strong. When she lay down on the river it had held her up and swirled her like a big liquid hand, and she lay on it, releasing energy to the sky, letting the river be the stronger thing.

"You taste like music," Richard says. "You taste like jazz."

It might be true or it might be a lie that there is only one part of her that is special.

"Jesus God," says Richard. His tongue is in her navel and she has stopped punching his head because she is thinking, she is in the hand of the burning river, she is rising hotly through the leaves, and she hears him make the long sliding moan of the trombone.

⚘ *Not People, Not This* ⚘

KELLY MAGEE

In many rural areas, there is nothing for a tornado to hit, nor anyone to see it.
— The Handy Weather Answer Book

In Alabama, a tornado touches down.

Within minutes, things begin to change. Tiny green tomatoes ripen instantly. Chickens lose their feathers. Whole cotton fields spoil; their curled leaves smell like rust. The blotch on the TV map turns blue to red in three counties. Cars scatter like grass clippings.

A woman in Montgomery opens her cupboard to find every dish cracked in thirds. A man in Mobile gets up from his recliner just as it bursts its seams, spews white stuffing into the living room. People all over the state report prank phone calls—hang-ups. Alarms engage for no reason.

Grocery stores in Birmingham sell out of raw hamburger, veal, steak. People growl. Animals murmur. The wind blows grills down the street, still lit, still smoking.

Here, storms make us believe things we never would on a sunny day. We'll accept weather as a defense for almost any crime. Like insanity, you can plead thunderstorm. Full moon. Tornado. We'll believe the lightning made you do it. That the clerk lost the money in the register. The wife just up and disappeared.

It could happen.

When the sirens went off in Montgomery, Opelika, a forty minute drive away, had already lost power. Residents emptied the main streets, and the parking lots of Kroger and Super Wal-Mart. Those who had basements retreated to them with flashlights and radios. WKKR reported the tornado to be somewhere in the country, headed directly for town.

In the lightless Whistling Dixie, two men listened to the weather report and toasted themselves with whiskey. They'd known each other from birth, but they were not friends. They were men, alive at the same time, who exchanged money and nods in the bar. One, Trooper, owned the place. The other, Ames, had been on his way out when the bar went dark, but knew an opportunity for free booze when he saw one. He'd suggested a last toast to the storm, and since their fathers had been neighbors as boys and their mothers still held Bridge parties together—and because, in a way, they were of the same stock—Trooper had agreed. Really, he wanted to be home, ushering his daughter and wife, who'd called the bar three times, into the basement, pulling a mattress over their heads. His own father had tied the family dogs down by their feet, but Trooper wasn't a violent man. Not anymore. He would pack the dogs away in kennels, let them howl and chew on the wire as they always did when the wind picked up.

The men toasted themselves first, then the weather. On the radio, the tornado played like a slow motion football game: yards lost and gained.

The second shot went down like bad blood. The sun hadn't quite set—in summer the daylight outlasted the day—and the

bar was light enough for Ames to notice Trooper eyeing him.
Ames knew that Trooper wouldn't make him pay for the drinks if
he caused a fuss. Trooper knew that Ames didn't mind screwing
his friends over once in a while, and they weren't even friends.

"There's nothing like a good drink in the dark," Ames said.
He worked at a pawn shop, but might've owned a bar himself,
had he gotten his act together in high school. He'd flunked out
because he couldn't keep his hands out of trouble. He had a thing
for the sucker punch. Everything made him mad, but especially
girls: the way they flipped their hair like it didn't drive him crazy.
And then, twice he'd gotten caught unzipped in indecent places.
Jacking off in the cafeteria bathroom, and a closet in the life science class. The principal had made sure Ames failed four out of
seven classes, the requisite amount. He'd left in tenth grade, got
hired at the pawn shop where he could pocket a little cash on the
side without anyone ever knowing.

Trooper raised his empty glass. Paused for tact. "Guess you'll
be heading home now," he said.

Ames held his glass in front of his eye. Trooper's face swam.

"Real nice," he said. "Really, man. Real goddamn nice." He
turned the glass on its side, aimed it like a dart at Trooper's face.
The bland voice on WKKR warned anyone on the road to seek
shelter.

"What's nice?" Trooper said.

"You're going to send me out in this." Ames aimed, leveled,
aimed. "Aren't you?"

"Yeah," Trooper said. "I am."

Ames threw the glass, but not at Trooper. He smashed it on
the floor. These days, he was given to fits of rage that didn't amount
to much. He wasn't really dangerous—not to Trooper, anyway.
He had the social skills of a mosquito. He wanted to be a better
man, but didn't quite know how.

"One drink," Trooper said. "You said one drink. We've had

two. Let's go." He was bigger, so he hauled Ames into the parking lot. It wasn't that he didn't feel sorry for the guy. Trooper understood Ames maybe more than anyone else. His wife said it was because of their proximity as babies. Really, it was because they both dealt with fear the same way: they hit. When he got married, Trooper developed a technique for disarming his fists: one finger at a time, five counts in between. He was aware how close he'd been to becoming an Ames. But now he had other worries. He had the wife and kid. He had priorities.

Ames, on the other hand, he lived in a trailer that stunk of gas from the stove and that wouldn't have a chance in a tornado. If he went home, he'd be surfing the roof in an hour. He'd be heading scalp-first for the nearest tree.

"Go home," Trooper said, and Ames thought, *easy for you.*

"I'm going," Ames said. Trooper backed his pickup onto the road, kicking up gravel dust. Ames toed one of the larger stones in the lot. He dislodged it, tossed it into the air. The wind was picking up. He had nowhere to go. Two years ago, a storm had flattened half his trailer park, and ever since he'd tried to find other kinds of shelter. But he'd run aground. He'd gotten kicked out of the library, state buildings, even churches. He had a temper. He couldn't help himself.

On the third toss, the wind pushed the rock forward in the air, and Ames had to run to catch it. That was the last thing Trooper saw in his rearview: Ames hurrying across the parking lot to catch a rock that, just then, seemed light as a bubble. Behind him, miles of abandoned fields—the Whistling Dixie's backyard. In front, the sky, still blue.

In Birmingham, weather was nothing if not conversation. Three out of every five families were on the phone. Grandmothers called grandkids up north—they worried. Parents called dorms in Auburn and Tuscaloosa, told their new college students to go to the lobby. People tuned their TVs to the Weather Channel, then dialed up somebody to tell about The Time. The Time crazy uncle so-and-so went outside in red flannel PJs to video a twister. The Time they found a cow at the intersection of Thatch and King, alive and mooing. Pencils through trees and trees through houses. Strip malls turned on end. Near misses. Almosts. Danger that made their teeth chatter when it was two hundred miles away.

"Obsessing about weather is a southern thing, isn't it," our friends in the north say. And it's true: down here, we're tied as much to climate as to place. We're up to our necks in it. But this is not geography, we tell them. This is realism. This is eight hundred confirmed touchdowns, this is ten thousand deaths this century. This is deviant meteorology. That's why the whole state pays attention. That's what we mean when—surveying the wreckage, giving a statement to the news—we say we've been saved.

We're not kidding ourselves. The sky, like God or Santa Claus, knows when we're asleep.

"The sky is watching," our mothers warned us before bed. "Go to sleep fast and it won't fall on you."

May called Judy, her neighbor, at five till eight. It took three tries to get someone to pick up.

"We were down in the basement," Judy's husband said.

"I just wanted to check in," May said, and her voice sounded older to herself. She always felt elderly when she was checking in. And she wasn't elderly. Not yet, anyway. "I'm leaving now for Saving Grace."

"Why don't you come over," Judy's husband said. "It's closer."

"I don't mind the walk," May said. Children were yelling in the background, and the thought of weathering a storm with a seven- and nine-year-old made her head ache. The children were fine, *children* were fine, but May preferred the company of softer species—the dogs she kept in her house that'd just had puppies. She'd had one little girl, long ago, who she'd since ceased to speak to. Her daughter would be thirty-two now, and lived out west. She'd left for college in Arizona, and returned queer. Literally. She came home talking about how flat it was here, how green, and by the way, mom, I'm in love with a woman. They didn't keep in touch. At times, May missed her. Especially in heavy weather. She'd checked the train schedule twice in the past year. Pretty soon, she'd be too old to travel.

"Anyway," May said, "I've got plenty of time. It's not even dark yet."

"Okay," Judy's husband said. "Be careful."

"Of course," May said.

She made a bed of towels in her bathtub and, one by one, transferred the litter of puppies into it. They were just opening their eyes. She kissed their wet noses.

"Good luck," she said as she shut the door. She knew people who loved pets like babies, but she was practical. She loved them like animals, which wasn't more or less, but different. And like animals, they had to fend for themselves. She, on the other hand, needed the help of the Saving Grace church, where the walls were sturdy and volunteers helped steady her nerves. She'd gone there for years. She knew when to leave her house by the way the clouds started churning. She gathered her rain slicker and boots, her flashlight. She looked forward to the walk—twenty minutes while the squall built up behind her.

Judy called just as May was walking out the door. They had something of a psychic bond, the two of them. Often, they guessed each other's thoughts.

"Let us drive you, May," Judy said. "Please."

"You know I like to walk." May surveyed the sky, looked at the clock over the kitchen stove.

"It'll take me five minutes to get the kids settled down, and I'll take you myself."

"Really," May said. "Don't worry."

In five minutes May would be halfway down the road, thinking of the puppies in her bathtub. She'd be rounding the corner where the hardware store was, halfway to Kmart, then the Whistling Dixie. She'd cut through fields until she arrived at the rear entrance of the church. By the time Judy had coaxed the kids back down into the basement, May would be knee deep in greenery. Soft clay staining the soles of her shoes.

"She's thinking of Ana," Judy told her husband. "That feud's got to end."

That's all there is. A bar confrontation, two phone calls. The evidence is hard to piece together—the tornado got most of it. There are missing person reports and police records and a bit of investigative work, but nothing that adds up to much. Except the stories, but those are harder to find. In Opelika, we're all telling each other's stories, but you have to know how to get at them. Nobody likes to think they're a gossip.

The tornado touched down, and it changed things. Afterward, May came up missing. Ames' car was still parked outside the Whistling Dixie, and one window in the bar was broken. Trooper found a rock on the bar floor. Judy broke into May's house when she didn't get a return phone call, and found the dogs still in the bathroom. Ames didn't come to work for a week, and when he finally turned up, his story kept changing. He'd gotten sick of his life and had headed south. He'd taken the bus to Montgomery the morning after the tornado. He'd hitchhiked. He'd stayed with friends he couldn't name.

A bar confrontation, two phone calls. Everything else, the sky sucked up.

When asked about May, Ames first said, "Never heard of her."

As for May, popular belief was that she'd been redeemed, taken body and soul into the lap of heaven. It'd happened to several of the town's great-grandmothers. Some people said Ames had killed her in a rage and used the storm to cover up his crime. The police said the two cases weren't related, and they warned reporters about unduly frightening the public.

"Nobody killed anybody," Officer Gary Scott said. "There's no evidence that even puts these two in the same place."

Still others suggested May might've gone to see the forsaken daughter. Judy, who could guess May's thoughts, kept quiet. Efforts to contact the daughter were unsuccessful.

Of all the stories about weather, this one's our favorite. In 1986, a tornado decimated the Saving Grace Baptist Church. For two years, the congregation held Sunday services in the high school cafeteria, pooling money and prayers. When they finished the new church, it was the biggest for miles around. Stadium seating, hundred foot plate glass windows, video screens on either side of the pulpit. Electronic hymnals. The whole shebang. Visible at night from the highway by the security lights shining above it.

In honor of the new structure, the members changed the name from Saving Grace to Resurrection.

In 1991, on a sticky night in June, a tornado demolished the whole heavenly thing.

Not to be deterred and thinking brave thoughts of Job, the congregation returned to the high school and prayed. They held bake sales by the hundreds, donated life savings. Teenagers washed cars until their spines ached. The Baptist Coalition and the City Council pitched in. Then, on the flattened remains of two previous churches, the third church rose. This one had moving sidewalks, a weight room, a chlorinated fountain for baptisms. They named it Perseverance of Saints. They were the saints. They hung

a wall-sized, bronze plaque on the front that said, A Mighty For-
tress Is Our God.

Of course, it was doomed.

When, in 1998, the Perseverance succumbed to a double
whammy of two successive tornadoes in the same day, the town
gave up. Half its citizens converted to Presbyterianism. Two years
later, a contractor was brave enough to build an open-air mall on
the site, and no tornado has hit it. Yet.

It's all true. The sky is watching.

One story says this.

As a kid, Ames' mother's friends had complained about him,
said he stared too much. Said he had bird eyes. He'd had trouble
with women all his life, he didn't dispute that. In adulthood, he'd
turned to phone lines. Sex lines. He missed the flesh and blood
quality of peeping, sure. Growing up, he'd liked to watch the spaces
women took up, the way rooms moved around them. He'd been
your average boy with binoculars until high school. He started
with phone lines after tenth grade, when he didn't have much
access to real women any more.

He'd gotten out of control, of late. He'd been having trouble
getting it up, and sometimes he paid for four or five calls a night,
for nothing. Just to hold his sad, tired dick in his hand and listen
to a woman talk. Then, two weeks ago, a girl had hyperventilated
right into the receiver. At first, Ames had thought—you know.
Part of the act. But no. She'd gotten worse. Wouldn't stop, wouldn't
hang up. She made Ames so angry he'd ripped the magazine he
was holding.

"Get off the goddamn phone," he'd said.

He tried to hang up and dial again, but she was still there.

"I'm paying for this," he said. "Get a fucking paper bag."

Breath.

"Hang it up. Now."

Breath.

He'd yelled at her, bent over his legs and *yelled*. Found himself growing hard, his hand working below. He put the phone on his leg where he could hear her infuriating wheezing. He leaned back and groaned. His fingers grew slick.

Turned out it was the best thing she could've done.

That was what made him nervous: he'd gotten off on his own anger. It worried him. He'd begun to have violent fantasies. Twisting limbs, pushing in throats with his thumb. Gaspings. Stranglings. He didn't know what to make of it. He vowed to become better. He knew most people thought of him as a Class A pervert, but really, even he had his limits.

One Lola Jennings of Huntsville will verify parts of this story, say, "I just froze up. I couldn't move, I could barely breathe. It was my first time, you know, doing that sort of thing, and this guy was just so creepy. He got off on it, for sure. I'm not in that line of work anymore."

The crime scene, had there been one, might've looked like this: a bar with a busted window, a ratty brown car, gravel pushed outward at a point cater-corner to the door, as if in struggle. But as it was, no scene, no crime. The earth absorbed it all: evidence, indignity. The redemption story took off like wildfire. We do this: tell stories. We imagine May was lifted out of the mire. We're not exactly covering up the truth, we're softening the blow to our souls. We blame weather. We make it so we can watch the news wide-eyed, virginal. People are not capable of this. Not people. Not this.

Montgomery, AL. A row of pine trees on West Magnolia Street have lost their bark, reports Edward Greathouse. After the tornado Tuesday evening, Greathouse and three of his neighbors found their trees stripped of all bark. Otherwise, the trees are intact. All vegetation surrounding the trees, including flowers planted underneath, are unharmed.

"I mean, there's not one broken branch," Greathouse said. "But these trees are naked as new babies."

Greathouse says he knows of no scientific explanation for the phenomenon. He is not religious, but says he does believe in miracles.

"I believe this was a sign from God," he said. "We've been personally blessed." He was unclear, however, on the exact meaning of the blessing.

The trees were each over fifty years old.

Alexander City, AL. In a small town in rural Alabama, a line of tractor repair shops was damaged by an F4 tornado yesterday. An F4 is one of the most violent tornadoes, and can stay on the ground for an hour or more. The businesses had been vacated, and there were no injuries.

One resident of Alexander City, Jim Curtis, claims the destruction happened minutes before the tornado hit. Curtis blames the Tractor Graveyard, a field behind the repair shops that houses old equipment such as balers, rotary plows, harvesters, and threshers. There is even a crop duster from 1942, and a windmill. No one is sure where the windmill came from.

"Them tractors came to life thirty minutes before the tornado hit," Curtis said. "I heard their engines grinding."

According to this report, the tractors spontaneously came to life and attacked the stores that had retired them.

When asked why the tractors might want to destroy the shops, Curtis replied, "I don't know. Maybe they wanted revenge."

May's wrist was thin. Ames admired it at first. He thought it looked flexible, bendy like a straw. May could feel the tornado in the ground before it ever came near. Her wrist was not nearly as flexible as Ames had thought.

We called him Uncle. We never knew his real name. He wasn't anyone's uncle, just a neighbor a few houses down. As a young man, he'd grown potatoes that were the consistency of sugar— grainy. As an old man, he sold his farm to a white corn company and moved into a trailer. He was the only person we ever knew to survive a lightning attack and a tornado both. The lightning made him mean. The tornado cured him.

People said he'd been a good man, but after he got struck, we knew not to go near him. He assaulted kids; he molested them. Later we'd call these Ames Problems, but that wasn't entirely ac- curate. Ames never hurt a kid. Uncle sat in a folding chair in his front yard for years, until he got his legs back. We never saw him go inside, though he must have. His wife would bring food to him. She said he wouldn't eat anything but white corn. We could get close enough to flick his ears if we crept up from behind, and he'd reach out with his cane and try to smack our legs as we ran away. We knew better than to get caught. If you got caught, you were doomed. You'd return home with bruises, maybe a bit rumpled in the pants. Our parents told us not to go near him. We couldn't stay away.

He drove his wife from him with that cane when the tornado came. Told her he wanted to meet it ugly face to ugly face. The police found him in a ditch.

"I wrestled that tornado," he said. "The tornado lost."

He was dizzy for weeks, but when he could finally stop his eyes from rolling, he was good again. He didn't beat anyone with the cane.

Dinah Beaman tells this story. "I'm going back," she said to her first husband, six months before they were divorced. They were living in Ohio. Dinah, like many of us, had moved away, moved back, moved away. There was something about the south she could never quite leave. She kept wanting to return to her roots, the clean, white stalks of them. But when she got there, all she ever found was kudzu. "It's just for a visit," she told her husband. "To see if something grabs me."

"In Opelika," her husband said, "something's bound to."

At seven fifteen in Opelika, the Watch became a Warning.

Sitting in his car outside the Whistling Dixie, Ames thought about being good. He was waiting for the tornado. His only chance was averting it in his car. If he could see the thing, he could beat it. He'd tried to get back into the bar, had smashed the front window with a rock, but his arm wasn't long enough to unlock the door, even if he stood on a parking meter. That last tornado had thundered by and taken half of his neighbors with it. He'd spent the entire time crouched in his shower with couch cushions over his head, saying, "Oh, shit, no, no," and pissing on himself. He was not a brave man. The experience had fucked him up royally, and he wasn't about to go through it again. He started having dreams about tornadoes giving him blow jobs. He'd had about all he could take.

That was his thought before he saw the woman: *a better man.* Then he saw her, and the tornado touched down, and things changed. The wind whipped her hair into spikes, plastered her windbreaker to her chest. He knew her, faintly, like he knew everyone. She was alone. She was thin and strong, his opposite. Once, before he'd been ruined by bullying fathers and bartenders, he might've married a woman like this, been a gentle man. He could see himself, arm linked with hers, pressing foreheads to the wind. Somewhere between that vision and his slumped position in the car was where his life had gone wrong. He reclined his seat and lay back, out of sight.

Rule number one: in order to be a better man, he'd had to stay away from women.

But May, breathing gravel dust and thinking of the animals in her tub, had seen him first. Or thought she had. She looked, saw a man; looked again, saw an empty car. She didn't trust her eyes. If there was a man, she thought, he was probably drunk. Passed out. Unaware of the rocking of his car, the wind, the radio that, as she got closer, she could see was still on. If she let him be, he might stay passed out until his car wrapped itself around a tree, or flew into the bar behind him.

When May peered into the car window with a cupped hand, she was shocked to see the man staring up at her. Then his eyes were closed. May rapped on the window.

"You okay?" she said. She didn't like this man. He'd been thrown out of Saving Grace.

Ames didn't open his eyes. He pictured the woman's eyes, blue as a row of detached corneas he'd seen once in the life science classroom. The corneas had been floating in baby jars of formaldehyde, but Ames hadn't been able to shake the feeling that they still could see him. No matter where he stood, the corneas seemed to be watching. It was one of the only times, back then, that he hadn't been able to get it up. Now he had that problem all the time.

May could tell he was faking. His closed eyelids kept trying to blink. He'd seen her. He hadn't been asleep.

He faked a yawn. He stretched his bare arms.

Eight o'clock: sunset.

The tornado was tearing the guts out of an old silo. No remorse for its owners, huddled in an underground shelter, listening to the metal wail. Later, the family described the sound as an explosion, but that belied the awful quiet that existed underground. The loudest sound was their own breathing. The father held the ears of his two boys. The livestock were singing.

Seven miles away, Trooper's dogs chewed metal. His daughter held a flashlight, read a woman's magazine that was too old for her. His wife's thumb moved repetitively over the back of his hand. His skin there ached, but he didn't withdraw the hand. He felt guilty about Ames. On the drive home, the sky in Trooper's rearview had blackened fast, and Trooper was especially sensitive to veiled forms of cruelty. He hadn't meant to be cruel. Still, when he'd come home and explained to his wife about the delay, she'd said, "Poor guy. He probably doesn't have anywhere to go." Trooper had felt immediately sorry.

He took his wife's other hand, and her thumb on that side began working, too. The mattress, once he'd pulled straight off the bed, smelled like detergent and made him sleepy. The three of them listened to the dogs together.

Trooper would back the cops later. He'd say May must've gone west. But his face wouldn't believe it. His face would say: take the worst thing you can imagine, and that's what Ames did.

Another story says this.

Ames held one hand over May's mouth, while he tried to get off with the other. He wouldn't have killed her in the act. He killed her afterwards because he couldn't do it. Because even that, the worst of his desires, had deserted him. That's when the real anger hit. He could almost fit his whole hand around her neck. He didn't believe she was dying, even when her tongue pushed out from between her teeth. He felt better when it was over. He didn't need to struggle. His head cleared.

May felt the tornado in the ground. She felt her eyes bulge out. Her body had gone into panic mode—accelerated heart rate, adrenaline—but her mind refused to follow. She was still on her way to church. She just couldn't find it.

Ames dragged May's body into the abandoned fields behind the bar. There were plenty of old tools lying around. Grave digging would've been hard work for a guy like Ames, but he was running on fear by then. The tornado was coming, and came, in fact, in the middle of the burial. When it hit, he lay flat on the ground, watched objects fly around him: trash cans, doors, rakes. The experience left him untouched. All the holes he'd had were still in place. He was still afraid. He still had to heap dirt upon a grave. He still, in the midst of it all, wanted to be a better man.

Crazy, that two girls from eastern Alabama would meet in Arizona. Hundreds of miles from the Mason-Dixon line, they'd created a life alone, without relatives. They figured it was just as well. They didn't get out of Phoenix much. They still ate grits, fried their vegetables, watched the sky. They got quiet when the weather changed. They had a small, tan house with too-green grass and a cotton field out back. Cotton was enough of a relative for them.

Ana often talked about the possibility that loving other women was the only way for women to save themselves. She didn't disparage men; she simply didn't include them in her equation.

Ironic that her own mother had deserted her. Ironic, but not surprising.

When the doorbell rang one night, they weren't expecting a soul. They were eating dinner. Jill got up to answer; Ana put down her fork. They'd been talking about the new irrigation system in the field, how it made the air in the house wet. Made the bread mold. Ana listened for familiar voices. Water droplets slid down windows, and the setting sun turned them red.

"Who is it?" she called to Jill. She heard laughing, a surprised sound.

"Ana, come in here," Jill said. "It's your mother."

"I'm on my way to church," May said when Ames rolled down his window. It was getting late. The sun was gone. May had shifted her flashlight around so the handle of it was free—a weapon, if she needed it. She slept with her doors unlocked at night, but she wasn't stupid. She watched Oprah.

"Okay," Ames said.

"Do you need help?"

"No," Ames said.

He'd tried to save her. He had.

May knew she should've left right then. She could just make it to the church. But she couldn't leave. He looked so pathetic, lying there in his beat-up car. He looked like he didn't know any better. May opened the car door.

"Come on," she said, taking his arm. "Let's get out of here."

"I can drive," Ames said. Her sudden touch made his mouth gummy.

"No, thanks," May said.

Ames let her hoist him out of the car, and it took a long time. She wedged one foot in the door, propped his arm on her knee, pulled him out. He went. He was sweating. He pulled hard on her wrist when she helped him up. She held onto the flashlight.

"Watch it," she said.

They cut through the abandoned field. May thought she could see the plants breathing. Not plants, but weeds. Gorging themselves. Lit, as if from inside. They heard a sound, like a highway. Then a train.

"Oh, shit," Ames yelled, trudging through the clay, "you stupid bitch. It's coming." He made a run for his car.

Perhaps Ames did have repulsive intentions. He claimed he

never had a chance to try, and people were willing to believe that. There was no evidence. Ames said he hadn't made it back to his car. He'd collapsed in the field, and screamed. He could only assume May had done the same, but that she hadn't survived.

Afterward, he was arrested for stealing money from the pawn shop. People were willing to believe the impossible, but not that he was innocent.

May held fast to the plants on her left and right. She smelled dirt and clay, and something metallic, like a rusty bicycle. The tornado was in the ground. It was not part of the sky, after all. It was part of the land.

She opened her eyes when things quieted down, and found that she was not in the field. She had plants in her hands, but she was in the middle of the thing. She could see straight up to the hole of sky. On the thick walls, rapid-fire lightning struck. In the vortex, mini-tornadoes whirled. They bounced off each other and the debris they'd gathered. May was airborne, and yet still. It was surprisingly bright.

May let go. She dropped the grass in her hands, and floated.

Some people say May was redeemed. Reclaimed. That she was holy.

Some say she moved to Arizona.

Ames went to jail for theft. It was a kind of relief. For days afterward, the air fizzed like soda pop. Every explanation he gave was different. He seemed as confused as anybody about what had happened. He had no sense for a story, and maybe that was his worst crime of all.

There are the puppies. There are the two phone calls. There is the way we're more willing to believe the impossible than the tragic. The way we understand more about each other than, maybe, we'll ever admit.

In Alabama, a tornado touches down. We imagine it's the sky's eye. We imagine it's punishment and redemption both. More drug bust than drive-by shooting; more sentence than crime. Afterward, the wreckage looks almost orderly. Mailboxes with flags still raised stand before leveled houses. The breaks in the wood are clean.

On the news, they interview all sorts. Those who lost everything there is to be lost. Those who were saved.

"I slept right through it," someone will inevitably say. "Woke up this morning to my alarm clock." Clichés will be invoked: slept like a baby. Slept like a rock. They'll all point to the same thing. That here, we lose consciousness easily. We close our eyes, and dream.

Miss Spam Maps of Vegas

LYNN VEACH SADLER

I was a waitress. Waitressing is honest. I didn't want to work for the "World Famous Mustang Ranch." Didn't want to "pull down" $50,000 yearly for letting men "pull down" on me. Pull me down. Luke was my husband. He should of known that. But Luke kept trying to get me to "use my tips to enlarge my tits." Luke said they'd hire me for Mustang II and let me "work my way up" to the main house. Luke was crude. Once I found out how crude, I didn't want children either.

I remember the exact moment I knew I was leaving Luke.

Luke stayed out all night drinking and playing keno. He'd lost his bouncer job. Reno was trying to tone up. Luke, like me, looked cheap but didn't know it. I was working on not looking cheap. I think it has to do with education. Not always. I discovered that Mr. Benny Binion couldn't read or write but was smart enough to go in with Mr. Nick the Greek and let Binion's Horseshoe become the home of the World Series in Poker. Educated people may not be all that smarter, but they look smarter. Or they're "over the top" and look like Mr. Einstein. It's like the difference between Area 51 and Area 58 outside Vegas. All the educated are aliens to the rest of us, but the Mr. Einsteins move into a world of their own—Area 58. The rest of us go nuts thinking about their possibilities.

But I was telling you about the exact moment I knew I was leaving Luke.

I opened up for Whitey at 5:30 A.M. Luke got home around 4:30. Expected me to make him breakfast. Half a can of fried Spam with four over-easy eggs. Exactly *half* a can. The least bit of brown on the white, and I had to throw the eggs out and start over. If the yellows didn't "shake like the tits on a real showgirl," I had to throw the eggs out and start over. When I tried out that old joke with albumen as the punch word, he knocked me half way across the room. Luke always does or did everything by halves. Anyhow, after that, we didn't talk at all from the time he got home until I left for Whitey's. Luke was right about one thing. I was trying hard to get above my raising. Really hard. I read and stayed in the library as much as I could and hid my books from Luke.

The morning I knew it was time to go, Luke was lifting the eggs with his fork, looking all under the lacy "albumen" for brown spots. I just knew the yellow was going to give way and run, which was just as bad as far as having to throw the whole mess out and start over. Anyhow, once Luke was satisfied his eggs were perfect, he stabbed each one to make four yellow rivers. Do you know how that made me feel?

Wonder why there isn't a more sophisticated name for egg yellows than "yolk"? What I was with Luke was "yoked." "Yoked" to Luke the Loser. Why couldn't I run? I'd thought that question many times before, but that morning there was an answer. Suddenly, the four yellow rivers became a gold strike. It was like the remains of the Comstock lode silver mine I've since been to see at Old Nevada and Bonnie Springs Ranch. I had a tintype made there and pretended I was four golden rivers chasing after and piling right over the top of Luke Fallon.

That morning, over Luke's shoulder, I focused on the Spam can. I swear it was winking at me. Like Las Vegas neon. I knew better, but I saw the letters on that Las-Vegas-neon Spam can dance backwards. M-A-P-S. Spam was "maps." If Spam could be "maps," I could be out of there.

If *Spam-equals-maps* wasn't some kind of answer, I made it one. I didn't say a word to Luke. As per usual. I left my clothes, took my secret savings, and worked my shift. When Whitey got in about eleven, I sat down in his booth with him and told him. I'd been with him over five years, and he wasn't happy, but happy for me. He didn't know Luke personally, but he knew Luke types. He told me I didn't have to ask when I asked him not to tell Luke anything when he came asking.

When I got off, I returned my library books, which I mostly kept at work to keep Luke from destroying them, and went to Las Vegas. I hired a friend of a friend-many-times-removed to drive me in case Luke tried to trace me. "Maps" had glowed like Las Vegas neon. Besides, Luke would think I'd get as far away as I could. Probably all the way back to Tennessee. He thought I hated Reno, Mustang, Storey County, and all things Nevadan because I didn't want to be an "independent contractor" for the Mustang. Actually, I liked the way it supported people who had trouble finding support, and I admire Mr. Joe Conforte and Commissioner Shirley Colletti.

Vegas had another appeal for me. I'd read up on it some even before what-Spam-equals and saw it as some kind of, like, poor man's education. I know that sounds stupid, but the Vegas people put all that glitter out there to attract people, and it kind of blinds a lot of us to what else is going on. I don't mean just that it kind of brings the whole world and lays it at your feet. Which it does do. Yes, in a way that may be tacky. But it—well, let me see if I can explain how I feel about it. Since I've been in Vegas, I've seen *Forever Plaid* at the Flamingo Hilton, and that group it's about come back from the dead because of this sort of break in the ozone layer. Well, it seems to me there's an ozone layer separating the educated from the uneducated, but that Vegas is this kind of break in the ozone layer that lets the uneducated, if they want to, get a look at the world of the educated. And I wanted to. You'll laugh at the kind of examples I'm thinking of, but that's OK. Once I knew what I was after, nobody could laugh me out of it. I'm thinking of the "Pair-O-Dice" Club. "MADhattan" at New York New York. Mr. Cook E. Jarr performing regularly at the Continental. The whole Holy Cow, where the slots are "Moolah." Even the "Pornocopia of Sex." The Let It Ride High Roller at the Stratosphere, which is the world's highest roller coaster. The "shoe" equals box in baccarat. *EFX* at the MGM Grand, which I explained my followers. Their big production is named that because it's just dazzling with special effects, which EFX is movie industry talk for. Understand, I've learned most of this stuff since I left Reno for Vegas. Anyhow, I'm thinking of the "Caviartorium" and "Snackus Maximus" at Caesars Palace. The educated nowadays call it "cheesy" and "kitsch," but it makes a higher world "accessible." No, Vegas isn't just gambling, magic shows, impersonators, rock stars, star stars, stars lending their names to places, comedians, prime rib, shrimp, buffets, and sex. You *do* know the Flamingo Hilton takes dogs from the pound and trains them to perform? The Rockettes are there, too, and they're always referred to as "wholesome." And Vegas single-handedly preserves the history of ventriloquism right back to the Greeks and the Witch of Endor.

Nobody in Vegas liked *Showgirls*, which made us look like a bunch of lap dancers and lap-dance-fanciers, but I thought when Nomi Malone learned she'd mispronounced "Versace" was one of the saddest-greatest things imaginable. I've thought a lot about that moment. Enough to realize that "lap" is "pal." Vegas is full of Spam-is-maps-type-things. Like, underneath the razzle-dazzle, it's just calling you to words. And words just send you higher or deeper. If you let them. Why, I could be as blind as Luke, I soon discovered. I hated keno because Luke played it. It wasn't until I got to (and *into*) Vegas that I discovered keno was Chinese, helped pay for the Great Wall, came to us with the Chinese railroad workers, and has yin and yang halves. From there I went on to the Dragon Noodle Co. in the Monte Carlo being designed by Feng Shui principles.

I found out "Pamplemousse" means "grapefruit." Mr. Bobby Darin named that restaurant. Mr. Wayne Newton, among other notables, eats there, and Mr. Darin helped Mr. Newton get started (and Mr. Newton may have helped Luke find me. But all that was to come).

Whitey called his friend Mr. Cohen here in Vegas about me. At the Center Strip Inn. In exchange for running the graveyard shift, I got a pretty good salary and a room and bath out back. I figured I could either kill the cooking smell or adapt. I did both. I used vanilla like they say the Mirage mixes with the oxygen it blows in to keep the gamblers from feeling tired. The phone was in the restaurant's name. If Luke was looking for me, he wouldn't have an easy time of it.

I picked my new name on the drive from Reno. My friend's friend, the driver, was interested in the radio, so we didn't talk. Besides, I've always liked to think over music. The name I picked was "Sal Sagev." As in Spam-equals-maps. Since I didn't want to be too obvious, I was "Sally ('Sal') Sagev." I could tell when people tumbled by the happiness in their voice—"You're 'Sal' Sagev in my book, Girl!"—which really didn't happen too much until things started at the PO. Eventually, I thought to tell them I would always be a lass at a "Las" for words. I had to spell it for most of them or write it out on their napkins.

I made my way to the main library before I prettied up my new room. I had dreams about getting a degree, at least from a community college, but I was twenty-nine going on thirty. It didn't seem realistic. No, what I wanted was something respectable *and* upward-looking. I was a good waitress, but I just didn't like the tone of "She gives good service" and its on-the-side smirks. Besides, most customers looked at you funny and sidled away to another waitress if you even hinted you read. I could get away with Mr. Stephen King, especially after his accident, and Mr. Thomas Harris and speculating on whether Sir Hopkins would play Dr. Lecter and Miss Foster Clarice Starling when *Hannibal* was made into a movie, but I got looked at funny if I forgot and said words like "Miss Jane Austen's *Emma*." Though heads did turn when I pointed out that Mason placed his call about Dr. Lecter's kidnapping through a "legitimate" Vegas sports book switchboard. I did, when I became known, explain about Dead Poet Books to keep people from confusing it with The Dead Poets' Society but still didn't tell many I went to the Enigma Café and Café Espresso Roma, where all the UNLV students hang out, for the poetry readings when I could. I did send people interested in Gothic-Vampire to the Café Copioh and The Wet Stop, which also has Vegas's only live reggae.

One of my regulars was a walking postman in those cute shorts. He was recently divorced and on the prowl, but I liked him because he tried too hard to make people like him. He was after everybody's favorite bubble gum waitress, but she was waiting to become a showgirl and wasn't about to be "roped in." She was close-mouthed about where she'd run off from but talked about the latest shows and everything going on Downtown and on the Strip, and I appreciated the education. Anyhow, when "Angel" didn't respond, Walt started spending most of his in-restaurant-time talking to me.

Walt gave me the idea of becoming a "Federal employee of the PO," but he didn't like it much when I joked about a "hazard bonus" for all the danger from disgruntled former postal employees. At first, I meant to walk a beat like Walt, though the idea of the shorts bothered me some. After Luke, I didn't want to give the appearance of anything remotely "showgirly." Not that the shorts of the PO weren't perfectly respectable.

Walt wasn't the only thing that settled me on postofficetry. He told me I might not have a chance because I was female but not Black, Hispanic, or Native American. He said he knew the tarot-card reader at The Beach who could probably create some Paiute ancestors for me, but I thought if the PO was all that liberal, it would be liberal to me, too. Besides, if I went that route, I would have been descended from the Anasazi.

To find out about the postal service, I learned to use the computers at the library. When I punched in "post office" on Yahoo and got too much in return, my eye lighted in passing on Miss Eudora Welty's "Why I Live at the P.O." Not that I would ever be Sister, but the story seemed to be another "map." If you see what I mean. Not that I would ever link Miss Welty and Spam.

I studied hard and passed my test for running the postal machine and all the rest of the tests and was put to work in the back of a branch PO. And sure enough, the PO's liberalness was another map. (It is not responsible for all that stuff on the Internet about charging postal rates for e-mail.) My branch didn't have any Hispanics working out front, and the ones in the back couldn't speak English. I don't claim to *know* Spanish, but I'd learned some from my customers in Reno and now Vegas. I always try to strike up a *meaningful* conversation with my clients, so I'd picked up a tad. I just love it. It purely sings. Even when Hispanics are mad about something, you can't get mad at them because it sounds like they're singing to you. And not just huevos rancheros and things like that. I'd learned about "comal" grills and "caqzuela" ovens at the Coyote Café, where I also fell in love with Mr. Kit Carson's etched glass with the coyote and horse eating at the restaurant and with that "Painted Soup," which seemed to go with "Painted Desert."

Walt knew several people working at my PO, and he told them I knew a lot more Spanish than I did, but I, when approached, did agree to try, and my efforts seemed appreciated. I don't want to be immodest, but people seem to take to me. I mean, I don't think I'm threatening. I never want to be like what I ran away from back home or ran into running away from home. (Meaning Luke). So I try to be pleasant and nice to everybody who passes by.

It all just sort of happened. I went to work out front near Christmas, and people just dragged in like Christmas was an even bigger burden than usual. I kept looking at them until I got to feeling about as low as a junkyard dog locked in a 4 x 4 junkyard. I wasn't going to have it. I'd gotten maps out of Spam, and I refused to embrace the lowdown. So, not being very original or anything, I started to sing. I sing sort of like a Fourth Tenor. For a girl, I mean. It was pretty funny. I'd like to have a beautiful voice like Miss Streisand or Miss Buffy St. Marie, but if what I had lifted people a little bit, that was maps-from-Spam, too. So I'd sing "Grandma Got Run Over by a Reindeer!" or "I Want a Hippopotamus For Christmas," but I didn't forget I was there to serve Hispanics and others with similar needs (as I could), so I added to my repertoire. Like "Feliz Navidad" and "Tish Hinojosa." The more people liked it, the more I did it. Which is about par for human psychology. (The class I was taking at the time was Intro to Psychology.)

We had a big sign in the PO promising no more than a three-minute wait, and we made people line up and wait until they were called up to our windows. But the closer we got to Christmas, the more people we had and the longer they had to stand in line. They got crankier, and so did we. When our manager took down the sign, the people in line started snarling. They were ripping a roar in short order. I finished my customer and, without thinking, called out: "Next, please, but only nice people. Un-nice people, go on to someone else." And suddenly, I wasn't just the "Singing Lady at the PO" but a Vegas phenomenon. A small one anyhow. People tried to change places in line to come to my window. If I didn't offer them some snatch of song or some smartlip tidbit, they'd ask me a question. I was getting worried I wouldn't have the answer. For the most part, they weren't wanting another Miss Landers or her sister or Dr. Ruth or Miss Oprah. They just wanted somebody to tell them something straight and simple. Like about the bear claws at Benninger's. Krispy Kreme Donuts (the only ones west of the Mississippi). Mrs. Zelma Wynn's bread pudding on the Golden Nugget Buffet. That we should never forget that Mr. Chin, of Chin's, created Strawberry Chicken, no matter who claimed it. That the Lady Luck Casino Hotel has a multilingual front desk. That was the one thing I could be, I thought. Straight and simple. But I worked hard at it. And as we went along, others helped me. How else would I know to pass along as the restaurants for locals the Sand Dollar Blues Lounge, Shalimar, Toto's, Viva Mercados (even if does use canola), Liberty Café at the Blue Castle Pharmacy, the Algiers Restaurant and Lounge, the Steak House in Circus Circus and so on before they were voted favorites in the *Las Vegas Review*? Walt the Walking Postman told me, for example, that you could get an instant urinalysis from the urinals in the Hilton. The dealers, floor girls, restaurant workers, people connected with the shows, etc. who became friends with me and Walt passed on things the regular tourist writer-uppers didn't know or care about. Like The Sahara was the only Strip casino where you could play pan. Like The Riviera was one of the few casinos that offered sic bo. People knew I was into Chinese.

Nevada was my adopted state, and I knew just about nothing about Las Vegas until I studied up on it. But I soon found out the locals didn't either. I guess they felt like Sin City belonged to the tourists and they baby-sat it. Which, if you think about it, is a bad way to be about where you're supposed to be rooted.

That was one reason I kept on at the restaurant. Good waitresses are the closest humans to fish. They have these sort of banks of fish gills, and information is constantly being taken in through them and being let back out. If you listen, and good waitresses listen, you hear more than a little. All these people who come in together over and over are fish schools, and they introduce you to what's going on in their territory. Then all these random strangers come swimming through Las Vegas from places all over the world, and you listen to what's going on in their fish schools, too. Well, you have to develop a sense of what to keep or throw back, what to let through your net. I wasn't setting myself up as any kind of Great Queen Neptune. I just happened to be where people talk and the kind of person people talk to or don't mind talking in front of.

And then there I was at the PO. It's like *the* information center. Or used to be before the Web. But a lot of people, like the regular citizens of Vegas, weren't into computers. And there I was. Another version of Spam-into-maps. It fell to me to reconcile the locals to the so-called "hyperreal" world the tourists took for granted. If you're New York, Rome, Egypt, Italy, Venice, Monte Carlo, Burma, Mandalay, San Francisco, New Orleans, a volcano, water and fire shows, a rain forest, Treasure Island, Camelot, a circus, and on and on, how can you be Vegas? Or, what is Vegas?

If you've come from "Gass" Ranch and you're noise, neon, Glitter Gulch, Sin with a capital letter, The Atom Bomb, Gangsters, Movie Stars, Boulder Dam that gets renamed Hoover Dam and then back-names some more, your destiny is linked with the rise and fall and mostly rise of gambling, and you're the Eighth Wonder of the World, what is Vegas? If you're the only city in the United States and probably the world that has to publish the phone book twice a year, what is Vegas? If you're named "The Meadows" and you're concrete, strip, Strip, and stripping and your fake Manhattan skyline and New York casino are worse because they're made out of that Dryvit that's driving people crazy, what is Vegas?

So, I kept boning up. And trying to share. I grew into a sort of poor person's version of Mr. Anthony Curtis, the great guru of gambling who writes the monthly newsletter called the *Las Vegas Advisor*. Not that Mr. Curtis doesn't tell you about bargains in food and shows and such, but he's still mostly for the tourist set. The ordinary people seemed to like me. Not the PO big wigs, of course. They wanted to shut me up as an embarrassment. People wouldn't have it. Eventually, I was rotated to the Big Time—the PO behind the Stardust Hotel at 3100 Industrial Road. Caesars Palace keeps trying to get me moved to the one in their Forum Shops, but UPS and Fed Ex are giving the PO such fits, it seems like I should stay.

I kept looking to do something meaningful for the people. Or animals. Take Sidney, that big grouper people liked to watch at the Mirage. It was before my time when he got moved to the Long Beach Aquarium, but I like to think I'd of been one of them demanding he was too big for the Mirage tank. Meantime, my customers at Mr. Cohen's and the PO seemed to think I gave good S&S. That's "simple and straight" irregardless of what Luke would think.

I certainly never expected to get into Madame Tussaud's. They won't even let in Mr. Tony Orlando, except for his ole oak tree and yellow ribbon, but that's because he had a falling out with Mr. Newton over money. He ought to of known better. Mr. Newton got his start in the Carousel Showroom of Sam Boyd's Fremont Hotel & Casino. They don't call him the "King of Las Vegas" for nothing. There's a boulevard named for him. Why, he's had more standing ovations than any other entertainer in the world! The real "King" didn't go over all that well here at first, though he made up for it by marrying Miss Priscilla Beaulieu at the Aladdin, which was later imploded. No relation. But he had a fabulous come-back and went on to perform ten years at the Las Vegas Hilton, which still has one of his famous sequined jumpsuits, and Col. Tom Parker's memorial service was held there, too. But the Vegas lights didn't go off for Mr. Presley. They did for President Kennedy, Dr. Martin Luther King, and Rat Packers Sammy Davis, Dean Martin, and Frank Sinatra. Will they for Mr. Newton when his time comes?

They put me in "Madame Tussaud's, Too," along with Mr. Orlando's tree and ribbon. Though, if I'm any judge, Miss Tussaud got my hair from Serge's Showgirl Wigs and not from its outlet, which I certainly appreciated and wouldn't of expected. Even if it was sort of like Luke wanting me to start in Mustang *II*, I never imagined he'd come to Vegas or go there and recognize me. I'd been gone from Reno almost eight years.

Afterwards, I called Whitey, who graciously did some checking for me. The scuttlebutt was Luke'd gotten into money troubles and split. Why Vegas I can't imagine. But then I'd picked it so maybe we were more alike than I wanted to believe. Anyhow he'd come to Vegas and maybe was just being a tourist for awhile. Mr. Newton was the star for Madame Tussaud's opening, and Luke had always had a soft spot for him singing "Red Roses for a Blue Lady." He went, and I guess he must of wandered into Madame

Tussaud's, Too and found me as "Miss Spam Maps of Vegas." I'd been in the papers a number of times, always careful not to let reporters get a full-on face. Luke didn't read papers and wasn't likely to know me un-cheap and post-office-uniformed.

I guess Luke took it as a mission to find me when he found my likeness in Madame Tussaud's, Too. By then, I had moved out of Mr. Cohen's into a house Walt and me had bought in Henderson. We wanted to be married, but I'd had to tell him the truth about being married to Luke. He wanted me to file for divorce, but I knew Luke was cottonmouth-mean and would of worried us to death or tried to make Walt pay him to give me a divorce. And Walt would of. He's that nice and that wanting-everything-to-work-right-for-everybody-or-as-many-as-possible.

But everybody knew about me and the PO even if they didn't know my real name, and Luke showed up there. Fortunately, I was off that day. Fortunately for me at least. Not so fortunately for Luke. The wrong people heard about him asking around. I might of been able to talk some sense into Luke, though Walt says I couldn't have.

Luke appeared suddenly and disappeared suddenly. The word about him appearing got to Walt and from Walt to me. I waited for him to show up. To bring me down. Nothing happened. Walt insisted we go, as usual, to the Celebrity Deli the next Saturday evening. A lot of the old-timers hung out there, and there was a lot of tale-swapping about bosses in general and pit bosses in particular and about the good old days of Mr. Bugsy and Mr. Hughes. That night, I could tell they all knew about me and Luke. For one thing, one of the waitresses, who were all pretty much middle-aged here, brought me a red rose. It scared me, actually. It wasn't just that the only place in town where women got a rose was Hugo's Cellar. It was that it was a red rose and I was a blue lady. Who knew what?

What had happened to Luke? I had nightmares about the possibilities. Buried quietly in the desert. Thrown dead into Mouse's Tank in Valley of Fire State Park. Locked into one of Mr. Bugsy's tunnels. Shot on a Vegas street like Tupac Shakur. Sold as hamburger. I knew he hadn't been kidnapped by Area 51 aliens. Luke was too alien for aliens, though I didn't mean to be unkind, particularly at this juncture in his life. Or death. Fed to the Siegfried-Roy white tigers. Drowned in the pool at the Hard Rock. I'd be able to tell if the underwater music suddenly went to "Red Roses For a Blue Lady." But the globe in the Center Bar was inscribed with "One Love, One World." Nobody there would kill even a sidewinder like Luke.

The letter was delivered by a man driving a rented (Walt said) black limousine. It was gold-edged—envelope and letter—and he brought it up the walk on a red velvet cushion. Walt said it was real gold. He took off his hat when he presented it to me. Walt had to call me to the door. The man had to place it personally in my hands. Walt tried to tip him, but he looked scared, protested, including with his hands, and went off down the walk a lot faster than he'd come. It was addressed to Miss Spam Maps of Vegas in gold calligraphy, also real according to Walt. The seal over the point of the envelope was in red. The letter said:

Dear Miss Spam Maps of Vegas:

This is to inform you that your husband, Mr. Luke Fallon, late of Reno, has met with an unfortunate demise and is your husband no more.

Please continue in your present line of work for the good of Las Vegas.

Most sincerely yours,

One of the many devoted admirers of
Miss Spam Maps of Vegas

There was a stamp like the one in the seal where your name would go in the complimentary close. Walt said it was very old. Said he bet it went back to Roman times.

Once I settled down somewhat over Luke, Walt pushed the wedding. But all our friends were divided on where it would be, so Walt said we'd do it twice. Unlike Luke, Walt *never* did any-thing *halfway*. Once at the oldest wedding chapel, the Wee Kirk O' the Heather, and once in the Candlelight. We had four Elvis impersonators, all of them our friends.

❧ *Who Is the Hardware* ❧

MARIANNE TAYLOR

From the minute we sit down it's more of the same. Gunther B., the alcoholic midget is right there in front of us. His portable Big Book has worn a faded rectangle into his back pocket and the crack of his furry ass is peaking over the belt loop of his Wranglers. This is why his pants are falling—the book is like a wedge, pulling down the waist as soon as he parks himself in the brown metal chair. It happens every time. I point it out to Dead Cathy— not that she hasn't already noticed. She looks at it, leans over and peers down into it, as if, upon closer examination, it may turn out be something other than the crack it always has been. Cathy rolls her raccoon eyes and nods her chalk white chin which translates into *light us up a Camel for Christ sakes*—as if a Camel were the only thing to carry us through this fractured landscape before us, this terrain of broken lives and shaking hands and black coffee oozing like oil out of the rancid aluminum drums. And shitty cookies too—broken red and green Christmas cookies that only the desperate succumb to. It's Christmas Eve and someone, probably Gunther, has hung a big gob of tinsel from the AA microphone so it looks, when I blur my eyes, like it's melting all over the podium.

So far it's a night like any other, Christmas or no Christmas. If you asked us now, at 8:30, how we could possibly end up on the street, all bloody at 3:00 AM on the holiest morning of the year, one of us might guess *drunk car wreck*? But that's not what happened. Christmas is what happened.

Cathy pulls a quart of Jolt out of her bag and twists the plastic cap. The soda hisses up through the neck and shoots like dirty Champagne all over her decomposing leather jacket. It lands, in foaming brown puddles on the floor around her combat boots.

"Fuck it" she says, too loud, and takes a big swig. As the bottle leaves her lips it makes a hollow pop and the neck of the thing now appears to be covered in axle grease because even her lipstick is black. Cathy doesn't believe in coffee anymore; Jolt has twice the caffeine of even the strongest coffee which is a mere 200 milligrams per cup. "Why screw around," is how she puts it. Besides, she got tired of mixing up the sugar and Cremora.

Dead Cathy's booze of choice was Old Grandad and I imagine she carried it around in her big canvas side pack much in the same way she carries her Jolt. Cathy would drink Old Grandad until she passed out on any given floor, thus resembling (especially with all the makeup) a drooling corpse. This was her reputation. So now, she's like a dead woman revived. She says she'll drop the retarded nickname, even the makeup, if she can stay sober for a year.

At 8:40 the chair of the meeting steps up to the podium; it's Eddie D., an iron-fisted ex-marine who's spent his entire life since Korea in and out of jail. We know his story inside out so when Eddie starts screaming into the microphone ALCOHOL WAS MY MISTRESS (which always happens between the second and third wives), Cathy sticks her fingers in her ears; she doesn't care what people think. Eddie D., he's like Hitler up there and when he's done the entire room stands up and applauds. What's even more miraculous than Eddie D. not drinking for fifteen years straight is how everyone manages to clap while still holding their cigarettes and knitting needles and Styrofoam cups.

In the front row ahead of us, next to Gunther B., is Martin P.; he's taking notes which is what he does at every meeting. He is cataloging alcoholic trivia—the painful confessions of the poor bastards up at the podium who are purging one humiliation after the other into the microphone: like who ran over the family dog in a blackout, or who woke up naked in a downtown phone booth. Martin gets it all on three by five index cards. The Old Timers have confronted him on his practices: "What is said in these rooms, REMAINS in these rooms." "I know," says Martin, "but if I don't write it all down, I'll just forget." And he has forgotten, time and time again. "Besides," he tells them, "My disease is waiting for me," and he carefully annunciates every word: "IT'S DOING PUSH-UPS IN THE NEXT ROOM." He knows how much the Old Timers love to hear the AA jargon reiterated by the in coming wounded. They slap him on the back and say "Keep coming," which is their way of saying *Sure, you're an imbecile now, but after five or so years you might only be an idiot.* Martin doesn't tell them about the late night rounds of Alcoholic Jeopardy that he hosts from his long kitchen table, which is how we end up on the other side of town at 3:00 AM. Martin even has a Jeopardy card on himself, it says: *All the beds at the Greenwood Rehabilitation Center have his initials carved into the headboards.* The correct answer? *Who is Martin P.*

Eddie D. introduces the next speaker. She's a new one, this Sheila, and Martin flips out a fresh index card. Straight away we can tell that Sheila walks the fine line between out-and-out mental illness and alcoholism. It's the misbuttoned Afghan sweater and the fuchsia lipstick. She's been talking for ten minutes now and has not mentioned alcohol once. In fact, she's not talking about anything in particular.

Fortunately or unfortunately, the bathroom is situated only

about ten feet to the left of the podium so whenever someone flushes the toilet it gets amplified into the microphone and it sounds as if the speaker is drowning up there, which is what happens next, only Sheila doesn't seem to notice. And just as the toilet begins its Olympic refilling process, a car alarm kicks off a siren medley right outside the basement window so all we can see are Sheila's lips moving up there. Cathy's got her fingers in her ears again, only now she's humming "Rudolph the Red Nosed Reindeer."

This is how it goes that night, the way it went most every night: the microphone could go crazy with static and feedback for no apparent reason and I considered maybe, the problems originated right inside the speaker's mind and bad reception is what it sounded like. We were, after all, at the mercy of this rolling dial and anything, really, could be picked up and broadcast through the one working speaker. There was, occasionally, that element of surprise when the goods really were delivered through the wires—an offering of truth so profound that the room itself would seem to loose gravity. Just a line or a word or a strategically placed pause could be the good enough reason we were aggressively waiting for. Even a Sheila could be the bearer of such a truth though by 9:25 Cathy and I can see that the odds aren't good. Dance of the lemons is what Martin always called it. Like with cable, he says, we have to be selective.

The toilet stops running just as the car alarm ends so now Cathy's humming is officially a form of heckling and Gunther turns around with his evil midget eyes and whacks Cathy on the knees with his Big Book. This is his standard procedure for hecklers and it isn't the first time Cathy's been whacked either. Clearly, it's time to go out for our ritual breather so we abandon our chairs and head for the exit. Huddled in the stairwell are the usual street people who stink of want and shame and the fifths they keep hidden in their white plastic bags. Carefully we navigate the valleys between their filthy coats to avoid crushing a leg or an arm—or even worse a finger. They come for the heat and free cookies and to show the rest of us just how bad it really can get.

Outside, the church steps are filled with others like Cathy and I who have decided to sit out what The Hardware is calling another fucking whack-a-log. No one knows The Hardware's real name, only that he has at least five different stories about how he lost his forearm. Then he'll show you how the hardware works—how his stainless-steel claw can open and close with the flex of his bicep. "Who lets these lunatics loose at the podium," he says, kicking the railing hard enough to make the iron hum. One of Hardware's Jeopardy cards reads: *He was suspended from his job and forced to enroll in an anger management program by the name of Temper-Tamers.* Last week when the facilitator asked him to plant his angries into soap bubbles and blow them away, he told her she was *a mental bitch* and now he's suspended from Temper-Tamers. The Hardware, of course, had everything to do with the 3:00 AM incident.

"Jesus Christ," says another guy—a little guy with a greasy ponytail, just the kind of guy The Hardware might have laid flat after last call. "The lunatics are enough to make you hang yourself," he says, and he's serious, he's not laughing or looking at anything but the streetlight when he says it. And no one tries to talk him out of it either by telling him to that *it's not so bad after all* because we all know exactly what the guy is talking about: it *is so bad after all.* Not that we thought it was going to be a ride in the park, but there was always that chance. It's getting close to 10:00 as we sit there on the steps, raw and furious with the world and everyone in it. Everyone that walks by has a better life than us: lovingly furnished homes with awaiting plates of steaming health food and open-armed spouses. Their children will awake

tomorrow morning with precious handmade gifts of gold maca-
roni and they will cry for the joy of it all. We suck, all of us. We're
sober and we suck and we don't have presents for anybody.

People slow down because they can't quite figure us out. We
appear to be linked to each other in a curious way—but how
exactly, some are unsure. We don't belong on the church steps.
We're not dirty enough to qualify as out-and-out vagrants; in fact
some of us are in suits. We couldn't possibly be the church choir
out for a break; if Dead Cathy doesn't rule us out then The Hardware does.

A woman with large shopping bags slows down and stops
completely at the bottom of the steps. She sets down her bags
and smiles at us.

"Are you…" She's pointing at us, waving her index finger up
and down as she's thinking, "are you all some kind of church
group?"

"No," says Cathy, her eyes rolling up behind the curtain of her
bangs, "guess again."

"Ummm, I know…" She's tapping her chin, "a bus stop! This
is some kind of bus stop isn't it?"

"We're the choir," The Hardware tells her, which is what we
always tell the ones who are brazen enough to ask.

"No!" she insists.

Then The Hardware walks slowly down to the bottom of the
steps, right up to her face and just stands there like he's about to
break the bitch in half. Cathy slips on her granny glasses so she
doesn't miss what happens next. "WE ARE TOO," he screams
so loud that people down the street turn around. While this sort
of exchange was not common, it was not uncommon either and it
has nothing to do with the blood that ends up on the sidewalk
later—except to say that The Hardware's BP most likely went up
as a result of it. Cathy has her fingers in her ears again because
this is what she does when people scream and the song she hums

is again the very appropriate "Rudolph the Red Nosed Reindeer." whose melody is so universally calming that all of us start in and hum along with her. The woman, disgusted, picks up her bags and continues down the street. If I were her, I think, I'd hate us too. It must be the song that leads me to imagine we are all the Misfits of Christmastown, which is the very first thing that happens that has never happened before. Gunther says that we should never label ourselves or others, that labels are for jelly jars. But this, for all of us, is the hardest thing to do.

"Nice call Hardware," says Cathy.

"Good job," says the guy with the ponytail, "not killing her and all," and he slaps Hardware on the back which only freaks him out more.

"Remember the Island of Misfit Toys," I say, but no one responds and I think it's because the Island of Misfit Toys is an off-bounds psychological region. It's sadder than the saddest story we've ever heard from the podium and I wonder just how much it has to do with all that happens later.

Through the window we see Gunther stand up and pull his Wranglers back up over his crack and we know the meeting is over. Like clockwork follows the sound of stacking metal chairs and Gunther shouting commands to stack the chairs in twelve evenly spaced rows of ten—not nine, not eleven, but ten.

"You guys coming?" Martin flips wind from his stack of trivia cards right into my face.

I look at Cathy. She is dangling her glasses case from the skin of her knuckles, demonstrating to all who are interested her high threshold for pain.

"Whatever," she says. But we all know how much Cathy loves to go to Martin's loft and play Alcoholic Jeopardy until all hours of the night.

We walk, the small group of us: me, The Hardware, Cathy, and a few other stoic recruits. We march on like a chain gang through the city streets, on towards the dark industrial outskirts where Martin's barely furnished loft sits waiting for us on the top floor of the Wee Chin Noodle Factory. It's 10:30 and the only thing that sets our walk apart from any other night is that it's snowing and it's Christmas Eve which makes all the pedestrians happy except for us.

Alcoholic Jeopardy proceeds as usual: "He won two Wilson Fellows before landing himself in jail for robbing a 7-11 with a water pistol." The place reeks of noodles, but after an hour or so I can't smell anything.

Cathy jumps off her bread crate and hammers her deli bell so hard it doesn't even have time to ring. "Who is Wilton R.! Who is Wilton R.!"

"Correct." Martin is the best host. As we sit around the plywood table, chewing away at the sides of our mouths, we love him for making us dizzy with greed. He slides Cathy three Necco wafers which he buys in twelve packs from the CVS. "You may choose your next category from the board." The board is the chalkboard for daily specials that Martin stole from the last restaurant he was fired from.

"I'll take Loonie Noonies for one hundred please." The categories are divided by particular AA meetings. Loonie Noonies meet Saturdays at noon in the rectory of the First Baptist Church.

"He," Martin slides a card off the top of the Loonie Noonie pile, "was a Springsteen roadie until he was fired by the Boss himself."

"Oh! Shit, OH!" Cathy is anguished by uncertainty but she rings her bell anyway. "Who is Jimmy O.?"

"Incorrect, Jimmy O. was a roadie for Eddie Money." Martin taps the card on the table.

"Umm…" I tentatively depress the button of my bell with one

finger because I know how much Cathy hates to be wrong. "Who is Harlon?"

"Correct—Who was Harlon B."

As Jeopardy continues we notice that The Hardware's game is way under par. Normally, he's a big winner here, but tonight he's way off. He's mixing up the rehabs, the hit and runs, and all the blackouts. When he chokes on Cathy's most famous card: *She…passed out in a Lilith Fair Port-o-Potty and had to be pried out with a crowbar,* he goes over to the window, opens it and screams— not a gesture entirely out of character, but one we'd never seen before.

In the street it is dark and cold and windy like Rudolph's sad little island where all the reject toys warmed their reject parts around the dying fire. The three of us are walking home with our clothes plastered like sails over the lumps of our bodies. The fleeting joy of Alcoholic Jeopardy has faded and now it's just cold. The Hardware is swearing because he's lost his one damn glove and he's struggling to zip up his jacket because he's 50 pounds fatter in his life without alcohol.

Before long, the streets fill up with holiday drunks because it's 3:00 AM and the bars have booted them all into the sidewalks. Many are singing, arm and arm, with their coats wide open and every other bozo is wearing a Santa Hat. I can see on The Hardware's face that he is crying from the wind but I know he is crying, too, because watching a fair-weather drunk is like watching a dumb kid wreck the only car you've ever loved. Cathy says they should be locked up, all of them, for celebratory drinking. The government should only warrant alcohol privileges to those with irreversible psychological damage. Not just any asshole should get it.

"Great idea!" The Hardware replies sarcastically and I know

better than to agree with him. "So this asshole here—should *he* get a license!"

The asshole at first appears to be simply another asshole in a Santa hat but here's where our Christmas becomes full of surprises. On the guy's arm is an elf with no coat at all. They are so drunk, the two of them, they are like one flag waving in the wind. We see now, the guy's wearing not only a hat, but the whole Santa Claus ensemble. The elf is all Playboy Bunny.

"Hey," Santa gets right up into The Hardware's face, "you want a Christmas present?" He reaches into his black sack and hands us three packages, each with a small bell and velvet bow attached. Even though we know better, I think we are each hoping for a gift that no drunk Santa at 3:00 AM could possibly deliver. We can't blame Santa here for falling short but we couldn't help but expect more than three doses of Hangover Helper. Our Santa is evidently paid and outfitted by an anonymous pharmaceutical company.

We stand there, Cathy and I, and watch The Hardware who looks again as if someone screwed off the top of his head and poured in an extra gallon of blood. He takes the packet, rips it open with his teeth and empties it into the wind like he's making some big ideological statement about Hangover Helper. But the wind changes as he's doing it and most of the contents end up in the folds of the elf's little cape.

"Dude," Santa looks more confused than angry, "what the fuck is your problem?" Santa has obviously failed to notice that The Hardware not only has a metal claw but is bigger than Santa and his helper put together.

"You don't want to know my problem." The Hardware gets his claw right up into Santa's beard, pulls it hard about a foot away from his face, and lets the elastic snap back into his face. "Your present sucks—that's my problem."

Then, as if launched by an invisible trampoline, the elf leaps up and attaches herself to The Hardware's back. With one arm around his neck she grabs at his face with her long red nails and starts twisting his flesh in every direction. With her other hand she's pounding the sides of his head and her heel is soon planted into the crotch of The Hardware's pants which brings him to his knees.

When they hit the ground Cathy starts kicking the elf hard with the steel toe of her boot. She is kicking harder than one person should ever kick another and just as I am about to jump in to stop her Santa pulls me down and I can smell the vodka on his breath which brings to mind my bastard father and I'm off. He's got me by the neck and he's trying to bang my head into the cement. I am choking and pulling his real hair and trying to dig my thumbs into the wells of his eyes like the androgynous gym teacher taught me in High School. That's when The Hardware makes a 360 degree swing, to build up momentum I suppose, and whacks Santa on the side of the head with his claw. For a second, Santa is stunned frozen, then he tips over and falls like a bottle.

I sit up, coughing and my neck feels like snapped elastic. Cathy's on top of the elf when she looks over and sees Santa with his face in the snow. He's not moving and his ear is all bloody. *Jesus Christ*, I'm thinking; I can see The Hardware's next card: *He...killed Santa on Christmas morning*. Cathy kneels down next to him, turns Santa over, and slaps him hard in the face with the elf doing nothing to stop her. When that doesn't work she takes out her Jolt and pours some straight over his forehead. Like magic, the guy come comes back to life.

I feel sorry for Santa, even though, minutes ago, he attempted to kill me. When he picks up his bag of Hangover Helper I am happy that no one states the obvious concerning how much he will need it. Our three captivated pedestrians disperse, as it's clear no actual murder occurred or is likely to. The elf takes off her little cape, fills it with snow, and holds it onto Santa's ear. I realize they quite possibly know each other's names—maybe even love each other.

Before they leave, The Hardware takes off his jacket and gives it to the elf—then off they went much slower than they came. I wonder if they will have sex anyway or just cry in each other's arms when they get to where they're going.

"Like those two," says Cathy. "They would be eligible for a license."

None of us laugh because even though the idea was a little bit funny it really wasn't funny enough to start laughing at with some of us still bleeding.

The Hardware started walking first. "I fuckin' hate Christmas," he says, pulling long white hairs out of his claw.

None of us could have said it better, really, and I think we all felt something close to proud for all the presents we never got. Here was the thing: this shitty life was ours and no one else's, and Santa, we just knew, would be sorry tomorrow.

❧ *My Last Days as Me* ❧

CHARLES YU

The new woman is not as good as the old one. Me doesn't like her and neither do I.

On her first day, I discover three things about the new woman:

1. She is too short to play My Mother.
2. She doesn't smell right.
3. When she puts on the fat suit, she doesn't look like My Mother—she looks like a woman in a fat suit.

This causes a number of problems in the Tender Mother-Son Interactions at the end of every episode. For one thing, because she is so short, I have to lean down, really almost crouch, just to put my face near her face for the close-up.

And when I'm that close, it's hard to concentrate because she smells so weird. If I can't concentrate, I can't make the face for Showing Tenderness. And if I can't make the face for Showing Tenderness, how am I supposed to properly evoke Tinged With Melancholy?

—

As Me, my primary job is to evoke Tinged With Melancholy, as often and as accurately as possible. For example:

Episode 4,572,011—DINNER IS REALLY GOOD, MA

FADE IN:

INT. FAMILY KITCHEN—EARLY EVENING

    ME
Dinner is really good, Ma.

    MA
No. It's not.

    ME
Yes, it is. It's really good, Ma. These beans are really buttery.

    MA
Are they too salty?

    ME
No, they're not too salty.

    MA
Too salty, huh?

    ME
No, not at all. Not too salty.

MA

Too salty. I know.

ME

(sudden, disproportionate anger)

No, Ma, they are not too salty. I didn't say that. Why would you say I said that? These beans are buttery. These beans are perfect. These are perfect, goddamned beans. They are beautiful and they are not too salty. Why don't you ever listen?

MA

I'm sorry. You're just being nice to me. They're too salty.

ME

Oh, my God, Ma. I just said. Oh my God. Ma! These beans are buttery. They are not too salty. Don't say sorry. I love these beans. I love them so much. I'm not just saying that. I know they're beans, I know they're just beans, and it might seem silly, but I really love them. Please please. Don't say sorry. Please don't say sorry again.

MA

Sorry.

ME

I just said don't say sorry. What are you sorry for? What could you possibly be sorry for? I swear, if you say sorry one more time, my head is going to implode.

MA

Sorry.

ME
(suddenly tinged with melancholy)
I'm sorry. I'm sorry I yelled. Why are you sorry? Don't say sorry.

MA
Sorry.

—

Just to get things straight: Me is sixteen years old. I am twenty-two. I have been playing Me for as long as I can remember. In that time, three boys have played My Brother and eight women have played My Mother.

I admit, playing My Mother is undoubtedly the hardest role on Family. When casting each new My Mother, I think they have tried to pick a woman age appropriate relative to Me and My Brother. The first one I barely remember, except that her skin was quite warm. The fifth My Mother was also very good. She taught Me to tie Me's shoes.

The most recent one, I miss her. She had started slower than any of them, during the Puberty Season. But she worked at it. She was always working at it. The technical aspects: Martyr Complex, Unbreakable Matriarch, Weight of the World. During her run, every show had a direction. Every gesture had a purpose.

Her last year was her best. That was the season Me finished high school a year early. My Father was written out of the show, the excuse being something about infidelity. The guy just wanted out of his contract. He'd been there for too long and didn't like where his character was going: the show's anchor, a stable presence, a jocular, asexual, Harmless Bearded Sitcom Dad.

That last season was the best in the history of the program. Me and My Mother averaged nearly fourteen Tender Interactions per week. Ratings for Family were at an all-time high. My

Mother cried Pitifully almost every episode. She had Large Problems. It was beautiful to watch her Suffer. A true professional.

This new woman, however, is not a professional. I realize that following her predecessor would have been tough for anyone. I didn't expect it to go on forever. I'm realistic. If anything, I'm realistic. But this new woman. She's out of left field. She's a complete stranger. I suspect that she has never played My Mother before in her life. For one thing, there is the smell. And, as I mentioned, she does not wear the fat suit very well.

Her first show is a disaster.

Family is in the middle of a six-show arc: Me gets a Love Interest, Me loses the Love Interest, Me learns a Lesson About Loss.

The scene we're shooting that day is just about the easiest scene she could have asked for. Me is expecting a phone call from the Love Interest, and goes looking for the cordless phone. Me enters My Mother's bedroom to get the phone.

Episode 4,572,389—HEY MA, HAVE YOU SEEN THE CORDLESS?

FADE IN:

INT. MY MOTHER'S BEDROOM—EARLY MORNING

    ME
Hey Ma, have you seen the cordless?

My Mother is lying there, dressed to go to the supermarket, on top of the covers.

MA
I think you left it on the kitchen counter.

ME
Thanks.

The scene should have ended there. The previous woman would have ended it there. But the new woman, she has ideas of her own.

MA
(openly needy)
Can you stay in the room?

"What are you doing?" I whisper.

MA
I don't want to go to the supermarket.
I don't want to go anywhere. I just want to talk to you.

None of this, of course, is in the script. I try to explain.

"There's no Interaction," I say. I make a vigorous hand motion to mime holding a script. I try pointing to an invisible page and shaking my head.

She takes this to mean I am offering a Tender Embrace. This is bad. She comes toward me in her ill-fitting fat suit, tears already welling up and smudging her makeup. Her face is a mess. I definitely don't want to have a Tender Embrace, when it isn't in the script, when it is early in the morning and her breath is certain to be odd-smelling. When I barely know this new woman.

It goes without saying a Tender Embrace in the middle of Have You Seen the Cordless is incongruous bordering on offensive. Me has done this scene a million times, and never has there ever been a Tender Embrace. Not to mention the Openly Needy. Openly Needy in the middle of an ordinary show. That's what bothers me the most.

ME
(pretending not to have noticed My Mother's open neediness)
Oh, there's the phone.

MA
(like a little child)
Can you stay for just a minute?

ME
(trying to avoid an Interaction)
Thanks for the phone, Ma.

MA
(like a little child)
Please?

Me turns and walks out the door. My Mother weeps softly. The director yells cut.

Afterwards, I go out back to have a cigarette. The guy who plays My Brother is there smoking in the alley.

"Hey man." He pulls another one from behind his ear and lights me.

"Hey," I say.

This is what I know about the guy who plays My Brother: his name is Jake, he smokes a lot. In Family, he plays My Brother, who is fourteen, but Jake is actually older than me. Exactly how much, I am not sure, but he has crow's feet and gets five o' clock shadow by the middle of the morning.

Usually, we don't say much to each other.

"She'll get better," Jake says, to no one in particular. "It'll get better."

"Well, it can't get much worse."

We smoke a lot. We don't say much to each other.

It gets much worse. The new woman seems determined to turn every Interaction into something it shouldn't be.

Episode 4,572,866—NO ONE IS GOING TO CALL MY MOTHER ON HER FIFTY-SEVENTH BIRTHDAY

FADE IN:

The sun is going down. Me and My Mother are alone in the house. Me is looking in the fridge. My Mother is pretending to read a magazine. The two are starting to realize no one is going to call My Mother on her fifty-seventh birthday.

INT. FAMILY KITCHEN—DUSK

    ME
(comforting tone tinged with melancholy)
Hey Ma. Happy Birthday. How about we go to dinner?

    MA
(not even trying to hide disappointment)
Thank you. You don't have to do that.

ME
(comforting tone tinged with melancholy)
So, where should we go to dinner?

MA
(barely concealed fear of growing old alone)
I don't care. You choose. Italian?

ME
(realizing comforting tone is not working, wondering what
to say next)
Okay. Italian sounds good.

MA
(unbounded terror at realizing she is being comforted by
her own child)
Great. Let me get my coat.

ME
(wondering what to say next)
I'll start the car.

The director yells cut.

—

I go out back to smoke. Jake is there.

"Was she awful or what?"

"I don't know man. You know? She's not so bad."

"She's not so bad? She's not so bad? She forces her lines. She
forgets her lines. She makes up her lines."

"You used to do that."

"Not like that. I didn't look like a deer in headlights. She's turning what should be normal Melancholy into something else. Something formless and terrible. No name for it."

"What are you going to do?"

"I don't know. Get her fired, maybe."

"Man. You gotta chill. It's just a job."

Jake is very good at what he does. He's much better at Being Him than I am at Being Me, and he knows it. I suspect he thinks he's too good for Family, that he won't be here long, that it's only a matter of time. I also suspect he's just a natural, that he doesn't have to try very hard at Being Him, and sometimes, I have to admit, that makes me mad.

They don't write many Interactions for Me and My Brother. A couple of seasons ago, we had a tense, Angry Brother-Brother Interaction, but not much since.

On my day off, I go to the park. The air is cold and imperfect, not canned like in the studio. Ambient noise drowns out my inner monologue. I don't have to hear the soundtrack to Family piped into the building in a continuous loop of faint music. I take out my pocket-sized writing tablet and a pen and place them on the bench beside me. At the top of the page is written: How To Be Me.

Five year olds are playing soccer nearby. More specifically, they are viciously kicking each other in the shins while a soccer ball sits unharmed in the general vicinity. Once in a while one of them will inadvertently kick the ball, causing a considerable amount of confusion. But mostly they leave the ball alone.

Out of a mass of yellow-green jerseys and purple-silver jerseys, one boy is moving swiftly and with more decisiveness than the others. He breaks away from the pack and kicks a low, squirting goal through the orange cones. The ball rolls to a stop a few yards away from my bench. The boys look at me expectantly. I kick the ball back to them, too hard. We all watch as the black and orange orb sails over their heads and lands next to a dog, who sniffs it.

I light a cigarette and take a sip of iced coffee from my thermos. The cold liquid spreads through my chest cavity. I can feel individual rivulets moving through me. I consider asking the boys if I can join them, maybe as goalie. The parents are still eyeing me warily from my over-exuberant kick. I want to tell them it was an accident, that I would like to play soccer with their kids.

I stare at the blank page.

How To Be Me
1.
2.
3.
4.
5.
6.
7.
8.
9.
10.

I don't remember why I picked the number ten, if it was optimism or just a nice, round number. Or maybe pessimism. Are there ten ways to Be Me? Why not nine? Why not a thousand? I think about calling my predecessor, but then I remember I don't even know where he lives.

The soccer game ends. Hugs and oranges all around. There is talk of pizza and arcade tokens. A round of yays and cheers goes up as boys pile into cars and utility vehicles and vans in twos and threes.

—

The next day we have a short scene. It has been raining since before dawn. Me and My Mother have been sitting in the house all morning, moving from room to room aimlessly. The house is completely silent. After a quiet lunch in front of the television, My Mother asks Me to teach her how to teach her to use the e-mail.

Episode 4,572,513—I AM A VERY NICE PERSON

INT. THE COMPUTER ROOM—EARLY AFTERNOON

My Mother is sitting in front of the computer, hands resting on the keyboard.

    ME
Okay, Ma. Let's try to send an e-mail. Who do you want to send it to?

Silence as Me realizes My Mother has no friends.
    MA
(pretending not to realize the same thing)
Myself.

    ME
Okay. Send it to me.

    MA
What should I write?

> ME

Something, anything. It's just a test.

She sits motionless with her hands on the keyboard.

> ME

Ma, it's just a test message. Write the first thing that comes to mind.

She types: I am a very nice person.

She's supposed to just type gibberish, whatever, anything at all. Not something pitiful and honest and childlike. Not something that makes no sense at all except for loneliness and hunger for love. And who is she trying to convince?

> ME
> (trying to avoid a Tender Interaction)

That's good, Ma. Now click 'Send'. See that little tiny envelope? That's your message that you just sent. Click on that.

She opens the message and reads it aloud.

> MA

I am a very nice person.

The director yells cut.

—

I've finally figured it out.

"She's a faker." I say to Jake. But Jake's half drunk and not really listening. It's ten in the morning.

"She can't do Tedium. She sucks at Anxiety. She sucks at Quiet Desperation." I pick up a dirt clod and hurl it against the alley wall. It explodes softly into smaller clods.

"Not everyone's, you know, a Serious Actor like you," Jake says. "You know?" He hiccups.

"What does that mean? What is that supposed to mean?"

He takes a long drag of his cigarette and looks away.

"Hey," I say, "what is that supposed to mean? Answer me."

"Look, man. I like you and I like you as My Brother. But, all I'm saying is, you know? I mean, just relax? With your, what do you call it?"

"Creative research."

"Yeah. Always trying to, I don't know, be whatever."

"Me. Be a better Me. What's wrong with that?"

Suddenly I realize he does not feel the same way as I do about our smoke breaks. Suddenly I feel very silly for thinking I knew this guy who plays My Brother, for thinking he took anything seriously.

We smoke a lot and don't say anything for a while.

"She's not Poignant," I say, finally breaking the silence.

"What's Poignant? There is no Poignant."

"She's not genuine. She's not real."

"Real? What's real? Just read the lines and stand on your mark and try not to miss any cues."

That night I proceed to get drunk on the set. I wake up slumped over the Kitchen table. I have a hangover that feels like someone let a cat loose inside of my face. Half empty beer cans are all over. Next to me is an ashtray full of Parliaments smoked down to the filters. I hear birds outside chirping like winged demons. I want to be one of them. Or, alternatively, I want to clip their wings and then shoot them all.

Down the hall, I see the new woman walking toward her dressing room. She stops in front of the door and looks at me.

"Hello," I say.

It might be the alcohol or the difficulty I am having in merely staying vertical, which is focusing my mind. But I realize I am looking at her for the first time. Really looking at her. Her makeup is scrubbed clean and she is wearing a tee-shirt I wore two seasons ago. It goes down to her knees and hangs off of her narrow shoulders like a cape. She wears sweatpants from Wardrobe. Probably My Brother's. She is so small and so mammalian—the texture of her skin, the damaged coarseness of what must have once been beautiful hair.

I ask her what she is doing there in the middle of the night.

"I can't sleep," she says. "So I came here to work. I want to do a good job for this Family."

I wanted to say how can you do this? What do you think you are doing? You can't state the premise. You can't just say that you are Sad, that you want to be Comforted. There are rules, and there are times and places and manners for Showing Tenderness. I wanted to say, don't say it. It's better if you don't say it. But she is so small and she is a stranger and all I can manage to mumble is "great job" not knowing what to do but lie.

"Thanks," she says, looking at me quickly before slipping into her room.

A week later, I show up on the set and the New Me is already standing there, talking to the writers. I guess I should have seen it coming. What with the new woman and her way of doing things and also the discovery of Jake and who he is and how little he cares about playing My Brother. I should have seen the direction things were going.

People in the crew look at me like they have never seen me

before—makeup, grips, guys I had known for years. Just like that, I am nothing to them, now that I am no longer Me. I wander around, fingering the cheese cubes on the snack table and smoking cigarettes, trying not to watch Me, but watching Me anyway. He's about the same height, maybe a hair taller, and has a sunken look to him. They're shooting Dinner Is Great, Ma. I see Jake standing in the corner. He waves and comes over.

"Sorry you had to find out like this, man."

"When did you know?"

"I didn't."

"I don't believe you." Film is rolling. Someone shushes us. We watch for a while. Then I see that Jake has been replaced, too. Some college guy, full in the shoulders, with the cuffs of his Oxford button-down rolled over his meaty forearms. He looks like he's straight from a catalog.

"This guy sucks at Tinged With Melancholy," I say, out of jealousy. And it's true.

"Yeah."

"I mean, he really sucks at it."

"Yeah. He sucks."

"What?"

"What?"

"You're thinking something."

"No I'm not," he protests. I give him a look.

"It's just that, well, I mean, don't get me wrong, you're good at it, you were very good at it and when it was on it was on."

"But."

"But, well, why did it always have to be Tinged With Melancholy?"

Then I see his point. A huge pit opens up in my stomach and my cheeks get hot and the tops of my ears, too.

The way the New Me says his lines, he hits Comfort right on

the head. His pronunciation of 'buttery,' his rich, liquid sounding of the word 'beans.' He is so good everyone forgets they are watching a show. It gets very quiet. Crew guys stop talking.

Already my fumbling attempts embarrass me because I can see My Mother is Happy. Already I wonder if she, if anyone watching, will ever miss my flawed puny experiments, my willingness to be Melancholy, to make an amateur effort to properly Love My Mother. My search for happiness through Sadness.

The New Me can't do Melancholy, but he can do pretty much everything else. He can do Tedium. He can do Ironic. He can even do Secret Joy. The advanced stuff. But the thing is, I get the sense he doesn't even know the names. He doesn't think: now Me should tilt his head this way and furrow his brow just so to Self-Deprecate, to Commiserate. He's past that. Where I play wobbly individual notes, he plays chords. Huge, booming, double chords, eight, nine, ten notes struck simultaneously, with differing amounts of force, all of it coming out together.

I wonder why did I always have to Tinge everything with Melancholy? Why did I think it was all about Interactions? Why did I always have to capitalize every Emotion? Why didn't anyone explain that all I had to do was lean down, crouch down and forget the script and ignore the weird smell coming from her and say, to My Mother and to the strange woman in the fat suit: I'm Sorry uppercase and I'm sorry lowercase and I Love You and I love you and I'm here, Your Son, a stranger, a guy trying to play him. We're all right here.

THOMAS P. BALÁZS writes and teaches in Chicago. His stories have appeared in *Big City Lit* and *The North American Review* and are forthcoming in *Beginnings*, *The Distillery*, and *The Sulphur River Literary Review*. He is a graduate of Vermont College's MFA program where he was nominated for both the AWP Intro Journals Project (2003) contest and *Best New American Voices 2004*. He also holds a Ph.D. in English Literature from the University of Chicago. He is currently completing a collection of short stories titled *My Secret War*.

ARIANA-SOPHIA KARTSONIS's poems, stories, and essays have appeared or are forthcoming in: *Another Chicago Magazine, Bellevue Literary Review, Bellingham Review, Glimmer Train, Hotel Amerika, Hayden's Ferry Review*, and *Painted Bride Quarterly*. "Sundress" is from her collection: *The Smallest Body in the House*.

ROY KESEY was born in California and currently lives in Beijing with his wife and children. His short stories have been or will soon be published in *The Georgia Review, McSweeney's, Other Voices, The Iowa Review, Quarterly West, Chapman, Prism International,* and *The Mississippi Review*, among other magazines. His dispatches from China appear regularly on the *McSweeney's* website, and his "Little-known Corners" meta-column appears monthly in *That's Beijing*.

GLORIA DEVIDAS KIRCHHEIMER is the author of *Goodbye, Evil Eye*, a book of short stories published by Holmes & Meier and selected as a finalist for the National Jewish Book Awards in 2000. Her stories have appeared in *New Letters, North American Review, Cimarron Review, Arts & Letters, Bridges, Carolina Quarterly, Kansas Quarterly*, and other magazines, Her work has been included in six anthologies, and broadcast over National Public Radio. She is co-author of *We Were So Beloved*, a nonfiction book published by the University of Pittsburgh Press.

Poet KAREN KOVACIK began writing fiction at the age of 40, and her stories have appeared in *Glimmer Train, Chelsea*, and *Quarter After Eight*. Now she's in Poland on a translation Fulbright, where having survived many gray December days, she is radiantly alive. Her next book of poems, *Metropolis Burning*, is forthcoming from Cleveland State University Press in summer 2005.

DYLAN LANDIS is writing a novel, *Floorwork*, and a collection of linked stories. Her fiction has appeared in *Tin House, Bomb, Best American Nonrequired Reading 2003*, and other publications, and has won the Poets & Writers California Voices Award, Ray Bradbury Short Story Fellowship, and Richard Yates Short Story Award. In a past life she wrote six books on interior design. She lives in Los Angeles.

KELLY MAGEE is from Florida but lives in Columbus, Ohio. She is a graduate of the MFA Program at Ohio State University, and her stories have recently appeared in or are forthcoming from

Marlboro Review, Indiana Review, Many Mountains Moving, Folio, Quarterly West, and others. She is currently at work on a novel.

The stories of former college president LYNN VEACH SADLER have been published widely and have won the North Carolina Writers' Network, Talus and Scree, *Cream City Review, Rambunctious Review,* and Cape Fear Crime Festival competitions. Twice a finalist for novels in the Florida First Coast Writers' Festival, she is also a poet and playwright.

MARIANNE TAYLOR's short stories have appeared in *The Boston Review, Side Show, The Southern Anthology, The Georgia State Review, The Ledge,* and others. Her first novel, *The Pathology of Love,* was a finalist for the 2004 Bakeless Prize, and she teaches Visual Art and Media Literacy in the public schools of Brookline, MA. She lives with her family in nearby Boston.

CHARLES YU lives in Los Angeles. He has published fiction in *The Gettysburg Review, Harvard Review, Alaska Quarterly Review, The Malahat Review, Sou'wester,* and *Eclectica,* and was cited for special mention in *Pushcart XXVIII.* In addition, one of his stories was selected as the winner of the 2004 Sherwood Anderson Fiction Award and is forthcoming in *The Mid-American Review.* He is currently working on a novel.

⊛ About the 2004 Robert Olen Butler Prize ⊛

The preliminary judges for the 2004 prize were Megan Campbell, Matt Dube, Chris Haven, and Anthony Neil Smith. They read over 600 stories and selected these eleven to be sent on to our final judge, Robert Olen Butler, who selected "News from my Father" as the winner.

Thanks to these readers and writers, and to everyone who entered.

DEL SOL PRESS, based out of Washington, D.C., publishes exemplary and edgy fiction, poetry, and nonfiction (mostly contemporary, with the occasional reprint). Founded in 2002, the press sponsors two annual competitions:

THE DEL SOL PRESS POETRY PRIZE is a yearly book-length competition with a January deadline for an unpublished book of poems.

THE ROBERT OLEN BUTLER FICTION PRIZE is awarded for the best short story, published or unpublished. The deadline is in November of each year.

http://webdelsol.com/DelSolPress

Printed in the United States
109130LV00003B/224/A